RUNNER'S WORLD® COMPLETE GUIDE TO

TRAIL RUNNING

BY DAGNY SCOTT BARRIOS

RODALE

© 2003 by Dagny Scott Barrios

All rights reserved. No part of this publication may be reproduced or transmitted in any form
or by any means, electronic or mechanical, including photocopying, recording, or any other
information storage and retrieval system, without the written permission of the publisher.

Runner's World is a registered trademark of Rodale Inc.

Printed in the United States of America
Rodale Inc. makes every effort to use acid-free ∞, recycled paper ♲ .

Illustrations by Robin Brickman
Interior photographs by Mitch Mandel/Rodale Images, except: Brian Bailey/Stone, pp. 82, 98;
Simon Bruty/Allsport Concepts, p. vi; Eyewire, p. xii, 8; Charles Gallung/Photonica, p. 50; Tipp
Howell/Taxi, p. 176; Chris Noble/Stone, p. 120; PatitucciPhoto.com, pp. iv, xii, 18, 36, 66, 105, 108,
144, 160, 200, 208; Tom Kirkendall Spring, p. 47; Anne-Marie Weber/Taxi, p. 48; Mark Weiss, p. 189

Interior design by Susan P. Eugster

Library of Congress Cataloging-in-Publication Data

Barrios, Dagny Scott.
Runner's world complete guide to trail running / by Dagny Scott Barrios.
p.   cm.
Includes index.
ISBN 1–57954–720–6   paperback
1. Running—Guidebooks.   2. Trails—Guidebooks.   I. Runner's world
(Emmaus, Pa. : 1987)   II. Title.
GV1061.B38   2003
796.42—dc21   2002155034

Distributed to the book trade by St. Martin's Press

2   4   6   8   10   9   7   5   3   1   paperback

Visit us on the Web at www.rodalestore.com, or at www.runnersworld.com, or call us
toll-free at (800) 848-4735.

RODALE

WE **INSPIRE** AND **ENABLE** PEOPLE TO IMPROVE
THEIR LIVES AND THE WORLD AROUND THEM

▼

For Bianca, my daughter—
may the trails always be there for her.

▲

Contents

Contents

Acknowledgments

Since my personal knowledge of trail running is anything but complete, this book is the result of dozens of interviews, conversations, and runs with experts who granted their time and wisdom most graciously. I thank all those whom I imposed upon. While there are too many to mention here, I thank in particular: Renee Despres, Tanner Dave, Buck Tilton, Brian Metzler, Adam Chase, Stephanie Ehret, Peter Bakwin, Doug Wisoff, Kevin Setnes, Scott McCoubrey, and Dave Mackey.

Thank you to the crew of editors at Rodale—in particular Leah Flickinger and Steve Madden—who did so well that unsung job that editors do: They made this a better book.

Knowing that my daughter was cared for by loving hands while I was hunkered in front of the computer made writing this book an easier task: Thank you Wendy and everyone else at Tinyminders. And as ever, thank you to my husband, Arturo, who never fails to support my running and my writing.

Above all, I offer thanks to the slice of mountain I am lucky enough to see through my office window every day. It stands impassively while I fret over subject matter and sentence structure, and reminds me why I run and try to write about it. Those foothills and trail in the distance pulled me out of my chair on many days when the writing grew stale or especially sloppy—and for this, I suppose, we can all be grateful.

Introduction

Let's start by dispensing with a few preconceived notions.

When you hear the words "trail running," perhaps you conjure visions of peaks to climb, rocks to scale, and endless extremes of hot desert and frigid snow. Or maybe you picture ultra runners looking lean, haggard, and bruised. And then there's this one: a runner 10 miles out, looping around in lost circles, finally backtracking at a walk to the starting point. Trail running certainly can be unforgiving at its outer edge of possibility. For the very serious trail runner, that's part of what makes the sport so appealing.

But trail running is not just for the hard-core. It's not just about climbing mountains. And it's not just for those who want to compete in 50- or 100-mile races.

For beginners and most veterans, trail running is about even more than that. Or more accurately, it's about less: It's less hazardous. Less exclusive. Less painful. Less extreme.

Trail running can be about quiet and relaxed beauty. A gentler trail will take you through serene meadows, on smooth footing, over rolling hills that don't even hint at a possible tumble. Running on a gentle trail is a peaceful meditation, uninterrupted by traffic lights or cars gunning past. These are the places to begin your trail-running experience. These are also the places to continue your trail running whenever you crave a pleasant break from the crazed routine of everyday life.

The catch is that once smitten, trail runners have a tendency to want to go further, both physically and emotionally. Once you've conquered the simple trail, it's natural to want to reach the deeper places the trail can take you. That's where the path gets rocky, the footing uncertain. You'll question whether you've taken on too great a challenge. You'll wonder what you were thinking. And of course, that's often when you get to the really good stuff, both inside you and out. You'll learn what you are capable of—on the mountain, in the canyon, and deep in the forest.

In this book, I'll guide you through the full spectrum of trail-running experiences, from that pleasant meadow to the farthest reaches of a challenging wood. If you've never set foot on a trail before, I'll take your hand and get you started. If you're already a trail runner and want to become more proficient so you can tackle greater challenges, I'll point the way. If you want to race, I'll share tips from some of the best runners in the world. And if you just want to read about trail running because you can't get enough of it, there's plenty here for you, too.

Why a book about trail running? I wish I could tell you how many people—none of them trail runners, I might point out—asked me that when they learned I was writing this book. On the face of it, trail running's an awful lot like road running. You put on your shoes and shorts, and you run. But how many times on a road run have you faced a downhill stretch that shredded your nerves until your legs wobbled out from under you? How many times on a road run did you lose your way and have to calculate options, hours, miles, and Twizzlers to find your way safely home? How many times have you run into a mountain lion on your local track?

The essence of trail running is about the unexpected. To do it well, safely, and comfortably involves more than putting one leg in front of the other. You're more likely to get too hot, too cold, or too tired on the trail. You're more likely to run just one more curve to see what's around that bend. And the great thing is, you never know what's around that bend. The road is predictable. The trail is not. Things happen on the trail; life happens on the trail. That's what makes it worthwhile.

I should make one thing clear right now: I am not a great trail runner. I live in Boulder, Colorado, surrounded by an endless "Who's Who?" of the best trail runners in the country. They call the Rocky

Mountains home, and for them, "Let's go for a run" means being gone for the whole day. My own experience is far less hard-core. Writing this book has been a humbling experience.

For me, trail running is the natural culmination of a life spent running. My story is fairly typical: I ran track in high school. I ran a lot on the roads in my thirties. Now in my forties, with my speediest days behind me, I want something a little easier on my body—and on my eyes. The trail fits the bill. I'm a much better runner than I am a trail runner. It's just that now I run on the trail as much as possible.

I'm probably a lot like most trail runners. These days my running is as much about escape and beauty, nature and nurture, as it is about fitness and health. I run on fairly straightforward trails several times a week. I wish I could do more extreme runs—harder, longer, more challenging—but I'm limited by my toddler's needs, my own work at the computer, and the other universal demands that always seem to conflict with the pursuit of a passion. In the end maybe that's a good thing. Chances are I'll be speaking your language in this book. I certainly won't be preaching from the mountaintop, literally or figuratively.

Use this book to enhance your own trail-running experience and avoid some rather silly mistakes that could cost you time, dignity, or a few small patches of skin.

Now lace up those nifty trail shoes you just bought and get out there. I'll see you on the trails.

CHAPTER ONE

Welcome to the Trail

Why It's Better Out Here

The trail I ran this morning I have run a hundred times . . . and a hundred times more. I have run it at daybreak, watching golden light filter through the trees to the east. I have run it in the evening, seeing the sun disappear behind the mountains to the west. I have run it in the heat of summer, breathing the sweet smell of hay and horses, and in the crackling cold of winter, the air so thin and hard it smells of nothing at all. I have run it in autumn, hearing leaves crunch underfoot, and in spring, splashing through wet, sticky mud.

I have run this trail slowly, pregnant with my daughter. I have run it pushing her jogging stroller for the first time, her eyes wide, giggles escaping at the wonder of the fresh breeze washing over her face.

This is not a special trail. It's not long or spectacular. It's flat. It's wide. It winds around stands of cottonwood trees and fields of cows, and it ends, unglamorously, at a road. This trail is not a challenge. It's simply the trail closest to my door, and the one I always come back to.

Today the trail was shrouded in fog that grew thicker over the hour until it turned slowly to mist, then rain, then snow. The ground was hard under my feet, but softer still than the mile of pavement that brought me there. To run on the road is a staccato one-two, one-two. Insistent. Hurried. Relentless. Once you reach the trail, footfalls become muffled, silent even, and instead you hear your breath. In (two, three, four), out (two, three, four). On the trail, the rhythm comes from a deeper place inside you—your lungs, your heart, and your head—as you hear your breath enter and leave your body. It's a slower metronome, and one infinitely more relaxed, than on the road.

On the road, your feet know every step they will take miles ahead of time—they can plow over the ground, mindless and oblivious. On the trail your feet are at the mercy of something greater. You must run softly, let your feet float, and then respond. You don't conquer the trail. You react. It is a dance and you're following the trail's lead. And as with a dance, the more you give in, the better it gets.

Trail running comprises a rapidly growing segment of the overall sport of running. Once considered a fringe element, trail runners now have their own selection of shoes to wear, magazines to read, and races to run. Why seek the trail? What do these runners find on the trail that they don't find on the straight black line?

A Connection with Nature

A road run tends to be about the self. We measure ourselves, we pace ourselves. We might want to get away from it all, and indeed we're outside in the fresh air. But reminders of the everyday remain: cars, traffic lights, railroad crossings. And the trail? The trail takes us away. The essence of trail running has as much to do with the outdoors as it does with running. And that means it's about something outside of us, a connection to nature. "I love road running and road racing—I love that feeling of going fast and working hard," says Renee Despres, an avid trail runner and writer who often focuses her pen on running. "But to me, trail running and road running are almost different sports." Despres explains the difference by describing an experience she had while running the 100-mile Western States Endurance Run. "I was running pretty much by myself in the early part of the course. I just looked up, and it was as if there was another voice in my head quoting a poem by John Keats:

Beauty is truth, truth beauty—that is all

Ye know on Earth and all ye need to know.

"It was this very spiritual out-of-body experience. It made me recognize the vastness of it all. I found a lot of comfort in that."

Despres, who happens to live in a place where she can walk out her door and choose any of six off-road options, says there's nothing like the feeling of hitting the trail. "I live in a kind of a dumpy little house. But I go out there and run in the Gila Wilderness [in Southern New Mexico] and I say, '*This* is my home.'"

Most of us must save the more dramatic trails for vacations, or at the very least, weekends, when we have time to drive to a destination. But there's a lot to be said for the trail just beyond the backyard, humble though it may be. You can run the simple trail almost every day; it can become an extension of your home. And it needn't be a bore. You learn every curve, the footing in every condition, the dogs and their owners, who waves and who doesn't. You learn the rhythm of the seasons: It's March, the cows are calving. It's July, the stream is low. It's October, the leaves are turning.

A Gentler Workout

Running on trails is good for the soul, a way to reconnect with nature on a day-to-day basis. Even if it's only for a half hour or so, it's worth it to seek the trail. But there are more grounded reasons to break the pavement habit.

Let's look at the trail from your body's standpoint. Concrete and pavement are notoriously harsh on the body; dirt, wood chips, crushed rock, and grass are much kinder. And it's not just your feet that get a break. The impact of running travels from your feet all the way up your legs and into your back. That means running on an unpaved surface gives your body a break from top to bottom.

The uneven nature of the trail is a bonus, too. That may come as a surprise if you think of ruts and rivulets as nothing but a sprained ankle waiting to happen. But when it comes to planting your foot, variation is a blessing. Here's why: Even the flattest trail provides bumps and swells, minute variations in the surface that you won't find on a road. That means your feet will land in a slightly different position each time they strike the ground. You're less likely to suffer injuries and hot spots from repetitive motion when you don't land in exactly the same spot each and every footfall. It also means you'll activate the tiny muscles and ligaments within your feet and ankles each time you land and stabilize your feet and legs. By engaging more of these soft tissues, you build and strengthen your physical support network rather than just pounding your metatarsal bones.

More Bang for Your Buck

Trail running is one of the best ways to build fitness for other sports. It's running with a strength workout thrown in for good measure. Running in general is widely accepted as the most efficient overall workout for your body. It generates cardiovascular fitness like no other activity, with the possible exception of cross-country skiing (but how many of us can do that in August)? Running is also exercise in its simplest, cheapest, most time-efficient form. You need run for only 30 minutes to an hour to get the same workout benefits as cycling for several hours, which also requires hundreds of dollars' worth of equipment. Even swimming requires at least a pool, a lap schedule, and a membership. No wonder so many athletes, from football players to rock climbers, include running as part of their training.

The drawback of road running has always been that it causes rather limited muscular development. While repeating the same leg motion over and over certainly burns calories, it doesn't build particularly dynamic strength. Trail running, especially when hills are involved, solves this problem by calling into play more muscles and requiring a greater range of motion. The more varied and rigorous the topography of the trail, the more muscles you'll engage in running it. Whereas running on a flat road can leave you with unbalanced muscle development, and surprisingly weak overall, running up and down hills will give you balanced strength by developing your gluteus muscles, quadriceps, hamstrings, and the muscles in your back. Throw in some obstacles to clear—roots that make you pick up your feet higher, a little stream to leap across— and you've got a dynamic workout, with the benefits of cross-training all rolled into your run. Trail running makes you stronger and will help you in any other sport you're training for. (And for that very same reason, if you want to compete in road races, trail running can only benefit you.)

A Slower Pace

Trail running provides a great workout, as well as tremendous relaxation. That may seem contradictory, but the relaxation I'm talking about comes from the "vibe" of trail running, which tends to be loose and cool. Trail runners share the sport socially and focus on enjoyment and nature. Unlike with a road run, you might find yourself on a trail for the better part of the day, running, walking, waiting for others, catching up, or simply taking it all in.

"Many people tend to gravitate toward the trails because they didn't like the hustle and bustle of the road running scene," says Peter Bakwin, a physicist by day who happens to hold the unofficial record for running the John Muir Trail in California. "They wanted to slow it down and have more fun and less stress about their running."

A Taste of the Wild Side

Few people will admit that they run trails simply because it's less stressful or kinder to their legs. After all, we don't generally do what's good for us, do we? We do what's fun. Ultimately, the greatest appeal of trail running is less about balanced muscle development and mental energy, and more about a decidedly unbalanced primal attraction we have with anything that pushes our limits and gets our adrenaline pumping.

Without going into a full-blown treatise on modern American social psychology, here's my take on the situation. So-called extreme sports and adventure contests grow in popularity every year, as do their audiences. Maybe it's because modern conveniences have so simplified the way we meet our basic needs that we crave more challenges. (Let's face it, feeding your average family no longer involves hunting down a woolly mammoth.) Athletic pursuits can fulfill our desire for adventure.

Now, for most people it's not realistic to re-create the Eco-Challenge on a day-to-day basis. A 9-to-5 office schedule doesn't lend itself to rappelling down cliffs in Fiji and then crossing gorges on horseback. That's where trail running comes in. Trail running can provide a sanity-saving dose of reality, minus risks to life and limb (and minus the intercontinental travel). "I think about trail running as another aspect of adventure," says Bakwin. "Trail running is a way to have those types of adventures without actually needing to go too far afield—I don't have to go to the top of Everest, but I can still push my physical limits. Within the context of a busy life it's hard to really get out there anymore; trail running is a way to do that."

The bottom line: It doesn't get any simpler or purer than running on a trail. It's just you and the dirt, the grass, the rocks, the leaves. Beyond exercise, fitness, and whatever confines you in your life, what could be more natural than running and jumping through the hills?

CHAPTER TWO

Just for Beginners

A Basic Trail Primer

Trail running is fraught with more uncertainties than road running. The weather. The footing. The way back home. It's no wonder beginners often have lots of questions. Here are the answers to some of the most common ones. With these key pointers and basic precautions, you can hit the trails with confidence.

Q: *I've never even run before. Can I start my running on a trail?*

A: Sure you can. Just use common sense. "Like any sport, you want to start at a level you'll be comfortable at," says Brian Metzler, founding editor of *Trail Runner* magazine. "Obviously, if you just started road running, you wouldn't do a marathon right away." That means keep it short and slow, and build up gradually.

Before you start, get a clean bill of health from your doctor, especially if you haven't engaged in regular aerobic exercise recently. It's especially important if you have a family history of high blood pressure, heart disease, or high cholesterol, or if you're over the age of 50. Your doctor will check primarily for heart disease, a condition that would require a more supervised introduction to exercise.

Once you have the physician's okay, a great way to ease into trail running is to intersperse a 30-minute walk or hike with periods of jogging. Jog comfortably and slowly—don't make the classic beginner mistake of thinking that running means sprinting. And when you get winded, walk briskly until you recover your breath. Then jog again. You can do timed segments—jog for one minute, then walk for half a minute—or just go by feel. The goal is to increase the amount you jog and decrease the amount you walk each time you head out. Start by doing this walk/jog workout several times a week, and as long as you build up your running segments gradually, you shouldn't experience significant soreness or injury.

Consider 30 minutes of nonstop jogging your first milestone. Once you achieve that, think about increasing your time on the trail. When you do increase your duration, do that gradually, too—by 5 or 10 minutes a run, and no more.

Q: What kind of trail should I start on?

A: As a novice, you'll want to look for a relatively flat trail with no steep climbs. Just as important is the trail's footing, which should be level and not complicated by rocks, scree, or roots. You may feel even more comfortable on a dirt road or a simple path such as one that runs alongside railroad tracks. If you're not sure where to find a good trail, ask at a local running or outdoors store.

Q: What if I get lost?

A: Don't let yourself get lost and you won't have to worry about what to do.

But seriously, coping with getting lost should be on an advanced runner's list of questions, not on yours. You can avoid losing your way simply by understanding your capabilities and working within them. For starters, when you're just building your fitness level and can run only for 30 to 45 minutes, stick to out-and-back courses on a clear, one-way trail, and turn around after 20 minutes or so. Choose a well-marked course, preferably one that's uncomplicated by intersecting trails. If you do run into unexpected trail intersections, note them mentally on the way out. Think of it as Navigation 101: Turn around and observe what that intersection will look like when you approach it from the other direction. Pay attention to the sun or large landmarks, such as a boulder, a bush, or a distinctive tree trunk, to gain a general sense of direction. Remember the obvious: If you head north on your outbound run, head south on the way back. And don't try going off trail or bushwhacking.

If you really want to try a loop course, be certain of the distance (walk it first to get a sense of how long it might take to run) and, again, choose one that's well marked.

Q: *Should I run with a companion?*

A: It's never a bad idea to run with a partner. And for novice runners it's a very good idea, until you're more comfortable with the uncertainties of the trail. "I'd say beginners and experienced trail runners should run with a companion," says Metzler. "If you're on a road and you sprain an ankle, someone will see you. On trails you can be isolated." Consider running with someone else particularly if you plan to go farther than you have in the past or will be running a more technical trail for the first time.

If you don't have a running partner on a given day, tell someone— a friend, your significant other, a coworker—where and how far you plan to go, and your expected start and finish times, especially if you're planning a long run.

Q: *What equipment must I have before starting?*

A: If nothing else, invest in a proper pair of trail shoes. If you already have road shoes, you might get away with them for a while, but you'll be more comfortable and safer in shoes designed for the trail. Trail shoes offer more stability around the ankle to protect against the dreaded ankle roll, and they have more protection underfoot and in the toe box to prevent bone bruises and hot spots. (Avoid hiking shoes or boots—they provide more stability than you need and will keep your foot or ankle from flexing properly. Plus, they're heavy.) Once you start comparing shoes, you'll notice different models designed for different terrain. Your choice will vary depending on where you live and run. (For more on choosing the proper trail shoes, see chapter 3.)

Depending on the duration of your runs, the only other item you may want to purchase right away is a hydration system. That's a fancy term for "something that holds water."

The general rule of thumb is to consume about 8 ounces of fluid for every 15 to 20 minutes of hard exercise. But people vary greatly; eventually you may realize that you need more or less fluid. You'll definitely want

Getting Hooked Up

Finding navigable trails and people to run with can be a challenge for someone just starting out. Here are some ideas to get you going.

No matter where you live, chances are you can find some sort of local trail-running scene. And if you live in an outdoors-oriented area, there are probably several thriving groups that meet casually to run. Even in a city, you may find a club that makes a point of traveling to trails to run. If your community has a specialty running shop (a store specifically for runners) or an outdoors store, stop in and talk to the employees. Someone should be able to put you in touch with individual local trail runners or a formal trail-running club. The store also may have maps, guidebooks, and race flyers available.

If you know of a trail race coming up in your area, go to it even if you don't intend to run. It's a great way to meet people and get ideas. If you can't find a nearby trail race or trail-running group, try meeting with a regular Road Runners club. Its membership may include other runners with an interest in trails, and you can discuss getting together or even starting your own group. Don't worry if you're not all the same speed. Social trail-running groups often include people of all abilities—the speedsters can push hard to the top of a hill and then circle back to reconnect with the rest of the group. You can find out about local clubs from the Road Runners Club of America Web site: www.rrca.org.

You can also find out about local trails from the Web site of the All American Trail Running Association (www.trailrunner.com). It's a great resource, listing numerous trails, with directions and descriptions, for almost every part of the United States. You'll also find race listings and other trail running–related events.

liquid available on runs of more than an hour, and many runners like to drink even on shorter runs. If you plan to run beyond the 1-hour point, a sports drink that contains carbohydrates and electrolytes will replenish your energy stores. It's always wise to err on the side of caution; as Metzler points out, "Sometimes trail runs wind up longer than you thought they would be."

A good old-fashioned handheld bottle works just fine, and you can buy hand straps that make it easier to hold. If you want to get fancy, there are plenty of other options, such as a fanny pack with a bladder. (For more information on hydration systems, see chapter 4).

Once you've made a commitment to trail running, you may want to buy some of the other fancy gizmos—a Global Positioning System receiver, say, or debris-shedding gaiters—in the outdoors store or specialty running shop where you purchased your initial basics.

Q: What else do I need to do to prepare for my run?

A: Know the weather patterns in your area. No matter your commitment to the Weather Channel, if you live in a mountainous or coastal area, know that conditions can change unexpectedly and rapidly. Wear layered clothing to adjust for temperature changes. Bring or wear a hat and lightweight rain jacket if precipitation is forecast. Some runners will even bring along a lightweight alternative: a large trash bag with holes cut out to form a neck opening and armholes. I'll talk more in depth about proper attire for trail running in chapter 3.

If you're driving to a trailhead, stash a few things in your car for after your run—a sports drink, an energy bar, a bagel or some fruit, and dry shoes and clothing to change into. Keep a small first aid kit in the trunk, just in case.

Q: Do I need to carry anything else with me while I'm running?

A: Always bring a little bit of food along with something to drink. Remember, for runs of more than an hour you'll want a sports drink that replaces carbohydrates and electrolytes, rather than drinking plain water. As for food, think sugar, salt, and low fiber. Good choices include pretzels, animal crackers, fig cookies, and sports gel packets. Experiment with what works best for you. (For more on fueling during your runs, see chapter 11.)

Beyond food and drink, your needs will depend on where you run and how far. A simple and portable first-aid kit for cuts or bee stings can come in handy. Renee Despres, a trail runner and writer who lives in New Mexico, always carries tweezers with her. "I run in cactus country," she explains. "Look at what hazards you might encounter in your particular region and make smart choices."

A small, lightweight fanny pack is ideal for carrying the few aforementioned items, plus an ID card and a little bit of cash. You can take your mobile phone for emergencies, but depending on where you run, it may not work. As an added plus, some packs have a special pocket where you can stow a water bottle.

Q: *What should I eat or drink before I run?*

A: Prepare for a trail run as you would any other run. And remember: You want to be neither full nor famished. Eat a light snack a half hour to an hour ahead of time. Carbohydrates and a little protein are good, but stay away from anything with lots of fiber or seasoning, as it can upset your stomach. A bagel smeared with peanut butter is an old favorite, or try a banana. If you've had a full meal, wait at least 2 to 3 hours before running, or your stomach may churn uncomfortably from the jostling and exertion. Finally, drink half a cup (and no more than 8 ounces) of water before you head out. But don't down a whole sports bottle, or you'll be making a lot of pit stops along the trail. The best way to achieve proper hydration for your run is to drink plenty of water throughout the day; that way you don't have to load up just before your run and find yourself with a sloshing stomach.

Q: *So, what do I do with my car keys?*

A: Take only the door key and hide the rest inside your locked car—you don't want the jingling of keys to disturb your commune with nature. Most running shorts have small pockets that can hold a single key. You can also buy a key pouch to lace onto a running shoe.

Don't leave your keys outside your car, such as in a wheel well or under a rock. Thieves intentionally target cars left at trailheads.

Q: *Do I need to warm up?*

A: Usually you can just warm up on the run. Jog slowly for the first mile or so until your body loosens up. After this warmup period, stretch any tight areas for a few minutes. It's best not to stretch before you start running because stretching cold muscles can lead to pulls and strains. (For more on stretching, see chapter 10.) The only time you may not want to warm up on the run is if you plan to hit very steep or technical terrain right away. Instead, jog on the road for about 5 minutes first.

Q: *I'm used to running on roads. How far should I run on the trail?*

A: One of the differences between trail running and road running is the way you determine the length of your run. Because the trail likely won't have mile markers, you probably won't be able to track how far you've run (unless you're very familiar with how different paces feel, in which case you can try to estimate your distance). It's easier to run

Trail Etiquette

Where to Park

Most trailheads have designated parking areas. Do your best to stay inside these areas. If the parking lot is full, look for a secondary lot nearby. Avoid parking your car on the side of the road on somebody's private property. You don't want to give runners and hikers a bad name—or have locals fight to limit access to the trails you love.

Trail Rating Systems

If you happen to get your hands on a list of trails in your area, that's terrific. Driving directions and trail descriptions can make things easier for you and allow you to explore terrain you might not have known about otherwise. But beware of trail ratings—such as easy, moderate, and strenuous—since these descriptors tend to be for hikers or mountain bikers, depending on the source. A trail that's considered a moderate hike may have miles of rock that would be much easier to walk on than to run on.

based on your watch. Shoot for a predetermined amount of time, running outbound for the first half of your run before turning around.

If you normally run for 45 minutes on the road, it's safe to assume you can run for 45 minutes on the trail—you'll just run a little slower and won't cover as much ground. Even though you'll be going more slowly, it will feel just as hard—or even harder, if the trail includes hilly ground.

Q: *What else do I need to know?*

A: Trail running is about more than getting from point A to point B as fast as you can. So before you start, consider adjusting your mindset—particularly if you come from a road-running background. Unlike the road, where you see the same scenery again and again, a trail holds beauty and surprises. Be prepared to stop, without guilt, when you notice something that takes your breath away—a fox disappearing around the bend, the sharp smell of creosote after rain, a Zenlike stillness in your mind. The trail even provides handy boulders to perch on during contemplative moments. So go ahead. Nobody's watching; nobody's judging. It's not a race, and you won't win anything by leaving nature in the dust.

CHAPTER THREE

A Different Breed

Shoes and Clothes for the Trail

The popularity of trail running has spawned its own breed of athletic apparel that has become popular in and of itself. Witness the scores of people wearing trail-running garb who don't actually run on trails—or even run at all. Rugged, outdoorsy sporting gear has become part of the everyday fashion scene, which means not all of it is engineered for true performance. So it's helpful to know what you're looking for in trail shoes or rain gear before you plunk down your credit card. Otherwise you may end up paying for a tough-looking, mud-colored ensemble that looks cool but doesn't run well.

Good trail-running gear is designed to take a beating in rugged conditions (just like hiking gear) while allowing for maximum movement and comfort (just like road-running gear). How much of this attire you actually need depends on your running habits—and your shopping habits. You may find that a lot of the running or hiking clothes you already have in your closet can double for use on your trail runs, especially at first, when you're not putting in too many miles and are traveling relatively easy terrain. The more serious you become about your trail running, however, the more you'll appreciate the unique trail-running hybrid.

This chapter offers a detailed look at the most common trail-running clothing you might want to consider buying.

Picking Out Shoes

The first question that springs to mind regarding trail-running shoes is "Do I really need them?" Chances are you already own other feasible footwear options, running the gamut from whisper-light road-racing shoes to heavy hiking boots. You may be able to run trails in either of those—for a while. But you'll be infinitely more comfortable, even safer, in shoes specifically designed for running on trails. So if you're going to buy just one item to get started, shoes are the way to go.

Before you decide to pop for those trail shoes, take a little time to get to know the terrain you'll be running on. Terrain makes a difference, because within the trail-running category you'll find shoes for different conditions. "Everybody's going to benefit from a trail shoe when they get out onto uneven terrain," says Scott McCoubrey, owner of a Seattle-area running store and formerly the trail-running coordinator for a specialty sporting goods manufacturer. "That means anything from foothills to mountainous running. City trails are really packed down, so you still can benefit from the cushioning of a road shoe. But with the variety of terrain in the mountains, the profile and protection of a trail shoe will make you more stable and protect you from injuries."

What makes a trail shoe a trail shoe?

A trail-running shoe is designed to protect you from the elements, such as rocks, uneven footing, slick surfaces, and moisture. Typical features include:

A protective midsole: Road-running shoes offer lots of shock-absorbent cushioning, but "in a trail shoe you'll find protection, like a flexible plastic plate in the forefoot so a rock doesn't come up through the midsole," says

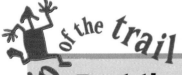

Foot the Bill

Running isn't a sport that requires investing huge amounts in gear, memberships, upkeep, or other expenses. So don't be cheap when it comes to shoes. Running shoes are expensive—and worth the money. You don't need to buy the highest-priced pair in the store, but you should spend enough to be sure you're getting good quality. Keeping your feet comfortable and happy is the best way to ensure that you'll love running for years to come.

shoe expert McCoubrey. That translates to greater comfort for a longer period of time on the run. Some shoe designs also wrap the midsole higher around the ball of the foot, forming a cradle rather than a platform, so that your foot is nestled inside for extra protection.

A lower profile: "A trail shoe should be lower and flatter to the ground, not as ramped as a road shoe," McCoubrey explains. "That gives you a more stable platform to come down on. Otherwise it's easy to roll over the side of the shoe." In other words, you're less likely to twist your ankle if you're not sitting atop 2 inches of puffed rubber and air.

Superior traction: The outsole and tread of a trail shoe are made from sticky rubber materials and use a lug design to ensure maximum traction. Some trail shoes designed specifically for running on rock employ

A toe bumper, lower profile, and superior traction offer protection from injuries.

A trail shoe (left) features a rigid midsole for greater stability.

composite rubber formulas manufacturers have developed for maximum traction on their rock-climbing shoes.

A supportive upper: A trail shoe's upper (the fabric part that wraps around the top of your foot) is more supportive than that of a typical road-running shoe. That's because it's crafted with sturdier construction or from stiffer materials, such as leather or waterproofed synthetic composites, as opposed to the light, breathable mesh of a road shoe. "Trail shoes are designed to hold your foot in place better," McCoubrey says, "and not allow as much side-to-side motion."

A toe bumper: On the road you're unlikely to stub your toe on a boulder, so the front of a typical running shoe is about as protective as a gauze pad. On the trails, it's only a matter of time before your big toe collides with an even bigger rock; that's why you'll find a thick, rubber bumper wrapped around and up the front of the shoe for protection.

Special features: Trail shoes come equipped with plenty of specialized features that vary from shoe to shoe—and shoe companies come out with new ones every year. (For a more detailed description, see "Terrain," on page 27.)

The Right Shoe for You

Running shoes are technological marvels, little customized race cars for your feet. They are designed for specific foot, body, and stride types. That means that a shoe that works wonders for one person can be an instrument of torture for another. With a little bit of research and smart shopping, your shoe choice can keep you running safely and injury-free for hundreds of miles.

The same biomechanical considerations that apply to road shoes also apply to trail shoes. But other considerations come into play as well. "On trails, the shoe's traction (the ability to grip the trail on the sides of the shoe) becomes as important as your biomechanics," says shoe expert McCoubrey. "You don't want to ignore biomechanics—it's still the most important consideration when buying a shoe—but other factors become as important." The most important considerations include fit, technology that's most appropriate for your stride, the type of running you do, and the terrain you run on. Here's a detailed look at each of these factors.

Fit: Your running shoes should be comfortable when you first put them on. There's no such thing as a "break-in" period; running shoes are intended to fit correctly from the start and not stretch or give with time.

Every shoe manufacturer produces shoes with a different overall shape. The form upon which they base this shape is called the *last*. The actual shape and width of the shoe should feel natural and should fit the shape of your foot. Try on several different brands to find one that does. Once you find a brand that suits you, like many runners, you'll likely become a loyalist. One brand isn't necessarily better than another; it just may be better for you because their last is a good representation of your foot.

When you try on a pair of shoes, feel for tight spots or bunches of material that press into your foot—add the friction of movement, and these pressure points will become a recipe for sore spots and blisters. The heel cup should be tight enough that your heel does not lift out of the shoe when your foot leaves the ground. You should have plenty of wiggle room for your toes—about a half-inch of extra space from the end of your longest toe to the end of the shoe's inside wall. This allows for foot swelling and ensures that your toes won't hit the front of the shoe on downhill stretches. Make sure the collar, the part around the ankle, doesn't rub uncomfortably against your ankle or foot.

Stride: Think of your personal running stride as a signature crafted by many different factors, including the size and shape of your body; the alignment of your hips, knees, and ankles; and the arch of your foot.

When you run, the manner in which your feet hit the ground affects just about every part of your body, from your toes on up to your neck.

Some genetically blessed runners have the kind of good alignment that creates a very forgiving stride—these runners could strap on construction boots and still run pain-free. Most runners fall closer to the other end of the spectrum. That means that the thousands of repeated impacts will eventually take their toll somewhere: on the knees, the ankles, the back, or wherever there's a weak link. That's where the right running shoes come in. Shoe technology is designed to compensate for problematic running strides. The two most common problems are overpronation (feet that roll in too severely when landing and pushing off) and supination (feet that don't roll in enough).

Overpronators have "floppy" feet and ankles: The arch does not adequately support the foot landing, so the foot rolls toward the inside

Trying On Shoes

Plan to try on shoes at the end of the day or after your run, since your feet will have swollen slightly. Otherwise you might end up with a pair that's too small and doesn't allow for variation in your foot size. Also bring along a pair of socks you normally wear when you run. Socks vary dramatically in thickness and your particular sock choice can easily change the shoe size you require. Finally, if you wear orthotics, be sure to bring them, so you can see if they fit in the shoes you're considering. It's not a bad idea to bring along your old running shoes, too: The salesperson can use them as a starting point to determine the proper model for you.

excessively, resulting in torque throughout the foot, ankle, knee, and even hip. Shoes for overpronators provide extra arch support and motion-control devices, in the form of stiffer construction, to keep your foot from rolling too far inward.

Supinators have the opposite problem. Their feet and arches are so rigid that they don't roll inward, or pronate, enough to provide natural shock absorption for the feet and legs. Shoes for supinators are more flexible, encouraging the foot to roll more during its contact with the ground. They're also softer and provide greater cushioning, protecting the foot and leg from impact.

Before choosing a running shoe, determine if you fall into either of these problem areas. Some pronation is perfectly natural and desirable. Ideally, you should land on the outer edge of your heel, then roll forward and slightly inward so you push off from the ball of your foot. Try a slow-motion walk-through while looking down at your feet, and you'll get the idea. Many specialty running stores even have treadmills that allow salespeople to diagnose your running stride.

Type of running: Ask yourself: "Do I run 20 miles a week or 50? Do I run at an easy pace each time or do faster workouts? Do I run for fun or to race?"

Runners who put in a lot of miles may want to spend a little more money to get a more durable, technical shoe. Lower-priced models are good choices for beginners or light-mileage runners who won't put as much strain on their shoes. Runners who do faster workouts will probably want a lighter, more responsive shoe for those faster runs. Consider keeping two or even three pairs of shoes to wear in rotation: a heavier pair for easy days of distance running and a lighter pair for faster workouts. Of course, if you divide your running between roads and trails, you can alternate shoes depending on where you run on a given day. Bear in mind that the longer your trail runs the sturdier a shoe construction you'll need. If your long runs last all day, your feet are more likely to sustain bone bruises and hot spots, so you'll want your shoes to offer the maximum amount of protection.

Terrain: Some trail shoes are designed with lots of rugged terrain in mind, others for slick rock, still others for excessive mud, sand, or even wet grass. You'll find shoes with a collar of fabric around the ankle to keep out sand and scree or a "lace garage" that tucks loose shoelaces away from twigs and rocks. Other shoes feature a waterproof lining. This makes them less breathable and prone to trapping heat, so they're better for cold-weather running. Still others employ a mesh construction to allow water to flow in and out. Such shoes are geared toward warm-weather running. Again, consider the terrain you run on as you decide whether these elements are for you.

Dressing for the Trail

Running clothes have come a long way from the cotton T-shirts and sweatpants of old. These days, if you peruse the clothing racks at a running or outdoors store, you'll notice lots of fancy fabrics and designs— along with lots of fancy prices. You're justified in wondering whether you really need to spend so much money for a shirt or a pair of tights— in some cases they cost as much as a pair of shoes—and exactly what you're getting for your dollar. Can you get by without the latest in fabric technology? Sure. Will you be happy to have it when you're caught in the rain? Double sure.

Three words of advice for dressing to run on trails: layer, layer, layer. If you've done any running or hiking, you're familiar with the idea. It's more important than ever on runs of more than an hour, during which you generate more body moisture than on a hike and travel to more remote areas than on a road run. If you're in an area with changeable weather, such as on a mountain, be prepared for whatever Mother Nature may throw at you.

It wouldn't be very practical to carry a bulky down vest or a heavy, waterproof slicker in your running pack. And that's exactly where all those fancy fabrics come into play. New technologies have made protective clothing less bulky and incredibly lightweight. One good wicking underlayer that weighs just a few ounces can keep you dry while you're sweating buckets. That's crucial when you get a bit higher up in altitude, the temperature plummets, you get tired, and suddenly you're not moving so fast and generating so much body heat. That toasty dry feeling is definitely worth the $75 you spent on the shirt or that feather of a jacket you can throw on once the rain starts.

The more you run, the more you'll expand your running wardrobe. For starters you'll want some good basic pieces.

Cold-Weather Basics

Underlayer: You want both warmth and moisture management in an underlayer. Look for a moisture-wicking fabric, which will pull sweat away from your body and pass it toward the outside of the layer so you don't get soaked inside. The same sweat that cools you so effectively by evaporating in warm weather can also lower your temperature dangerously, even on mild days. The risk arises when you slow your pace or take a break and no longer generate as much body heat—your sweat becomes an unwelcome air-conditioner that can lead to hypothermia. A long underwear–style bottom is a good bet for very cold weather, and you'll definitely want a long-sleeved top. Look for a zippered mock turtleneck if you want more protection around your neck than your jacket offers.

Middle layer: The purpose of a middle layer is insulation, which in turn will create warmth. It does this by trapping air between the underlayer and outer layer, allowing your body heat to keep you warm. Because you already generate a lot of heat when you're running, you'll need this additional layer only on the coldest days.

Look for maximum warmth and minimum bulk in a middle layer. Synthetic fleece works well because it's great at trapping air. This soft fabric has evolved over time, becoming thinner and more comfortable (and easier to fit under jackets) while offering the same insulating properties as its bulkier predecessors. If you want to get more use out of your fleece, spend the extra money for wind-resistant fleece—you'll be able to wear it in more circumstances and without an additional outer layer.

In most circumstances you need an insulating layer only for your upper body. You could wear fleece tights as a middle layer for your legs, but they're too bulky for most runners. Also, your legs require less help keeping warm than your torso.

Outer layer (pants and jacket): This layer protects you from rain, snow, and wind. You'll want a breathable fabric that also provides optimal water resistance. This is the place to spend a little more money on extras for comfort and convenience, including: ankles and wrists that zipper or snap for easy entry and exit; a neck that snaps tight enough to keep air out and is lined in a soft fabric that won't chafe; plenty of easy-access pockets; venting capabilities; and a longer fit in the back of the jacket. These layers aren't cheap, but when it comes to safety and comfort, it's worth it to spend a little more and get the best.

Once you've made this investment, you'll want to care for it properly. Water resistance can be diminished by machine washing or drying, so read and follow washing instructions to get the longest life from your outer layers.

Tights: For the trail, look for tights made from a thick, durable material. And again, choose a wicking fabric that allows your legs to breathe. Old-fashioned slinky tights have been replaced by more technical fabrics spun to look and feel like soft, brushed cotton while still providing excellent water-shedding capability. The legs should be long enough to cover your ankles, and the material in the crotch shouldn't ride so low that it restricts your stride. A drawstring is a nice added touch, as is a small pocket in the front or back.

Vest: A vest is a terrific addition to your arsenal against the elements. Vests offer just a little bit of warmth and protection where you need it most—around your torso—and are a great choice when the weather is just a bit cool, but not cold enough to warrant a jacket. Many vests are vented, with mesh panels or slits, making them even more versatile.

Hat: Wear a fabric that allows moisture to escape, since your head generates significant amounts of sweat. Fleece, wool, and wool blends are all popular choices. If you go with wool, look for a synthetic lining or band where the hat meets your forehead and ears; otherwise, those areas will get

Trail Etiquette

Castoff Courtesy

Many runners don't like to be weighed down carrying extra items, and when they get warm and strip off layers, they'll leave them in a conspicuous spot along the trail for later retrieval. So don't help yourself to that nice fleece sweater along the way; someone is planning to pick it up on the way back. On the other hand, if you see something lying along the trail getting trod upon and muddied up, chances are a runner or hiker dropped it unintentionally. It's a nice gesture to pick it up and hang it on a nearby branch or place it on a rock for the owner to find on the return trip.

uncomfortably itchy once you start sweating. In very cold temperatures earflaps can be a bonus.

Warm-Weather Basics

Shirt: When you're running in the heat, a shirt will protect you from sun exposure and ultimately keep you cooler than if you were running without one. You'll probably want a selection of sleeveless, short-sleeved, and long-sleeved models. Look for wicking fabric and an airy construction. Some feature built-in sun protection—you'll pay extra, but it may be worth it depending on where you run.

Shorts: Trail-running shorts are essentially a cross between hiking shorts and conventional running shorts. They have more pockets than plain running shorts, so they're great for stashing small items on long runs, and they're constructed of more durable material, so they're less likely to rip on underbrush or an abrasive surface. Many trail shorts feature the added protection of a longer inseam than their skimpier road-running cousins. Finally, they're more likely to have a drawstring: An elastic waistband can snag on brush and get pulled away, but a tied cord just may help keep your shorts on. Look for shorts constructed of quick-drying, lightweight fabric—usually some form of polyester, nylon, or Lycra. Most running shorts, but not all trail shorts, have an inner liner that takes the place of underwear. Many runners appreciate the convenience of this inner layer; just be sure it fits well and doesn't ride up as you move around.

Hat: Wear a hat with a brim to keep the sun off your face and head without contributing additional warmth. The good old-fashioned baseball cap style is superior to a visor, which does not protect the top of your head. Choose a cap designed specifically for runners, with mesh panels or super-light materials to encourage airflow around your head. If there's no shade where you run, consider wearing a hat with neck flaps for additional sun protection. On overcast days a brimmed cap can also help keep rain out of your eyes.

Rain gear: Choose a light, water-resistant jacket that offers protection against the rain without adding too much warmth in the summer months. It should fold up small and fit into your fanny pack. You're not looking for a lot of bells and whistles here, just a minimal protective layer. It can also offer protection should the wind pick up while you're out on the trail. Some runners have been known to save a few bucks on rain gear and instead pack an oversize garbage bag: Cut out holes for your head and arms and you've got waterproof protection at a bargain price.

Other Trail-Running Necessities

Socks: Look for high-tech fabrics (not cotton) that will wick away moisture. Since the demands of trail running often cause blisters, test a few different types of socks to see which work best for you. Some feature a double layer of fabric to keep blisters at bay. That way, any rubbing occurs between the two layers of sock, not between the sock and your foot. Also, seamless socks provide fewer points of friction and thus less potential for blisters. Thick or thin is largely a matter of personal preference; just be certain your shoe still fits correctly with whatever sock you wear.

Gloves: Your glove choice depends on how dramatic a course you run. Some runners just need gloves for basic warmth, while others need protection against abrasions. If it's warmth you seek, look for fleecy insulation combined with some sort of moisture resistance or wicking ability. An added outer layer that repels rain and wind is key in very cold weather. You can purchase gloves with an inner warmth layer and an outer waterproof layer attached, or you can create your own by layering a pair of gloves with a water- and wind-resistant shell mitten. While gloves offer superior maneuverability, runners whose fingers tend to get cold may prefer the comfort of mittens. Unlike gloves, mittens let you hold your fingers together so your body heat can keep them warm. If you need to grab something from your pack or your pockets, however, you'll have to pull off the mittens. Many runners like to wear a glove layer even if it's warm enough to be running in shorts, so consider buying lightweight gloves as well as heavier winter gloves. If you're running in a warmer climate, you may want to wear gloves for protection in the event of a fall. Cycling gloves are a great choice, since they offer padding in the palm and are otherwise airy and cool.

Sunglasses: Good glasses do more than shield you from the sun's bright glare. They protect your eyes from long-term UV radiation damage, errant bugs, sand, and even wind. Wearing sunglasses may take a little bit of getting used to, but it's a good idea to wear them on just about all your runs. For cloudier days, shades are available in lighter colors.

When choosing glasses, the most important feature to look for is UV protection. Too much exposure to UV radiation can damage the eye and may ultimately lead to cataracts. You can't judge the protection level of a pair of sunglasses by the color of the shade: Some very dark tints provide very little protection. (Protection comes from filtering the light, which is accomplished by a chemical coating that's applied to the lenses.) Check the label for the level of UV protection: Glasses labeled "Special Purpose" offer the strongest protection, blocking 99 to 100 percent of UVA and UVB radiation. "General Use" means the lenses block 95 percent of UVB rays and 60 percent of UVA. Glasses labeled "Cosmetic" offer only 70 percent protection from UVB rays.

While you're at it, look for a style that wraps around your eyes generously; these larger sizes keep out sun and bugs from the sides as well as from the front. When trying on glasses, prop them up on your head to see if they'll stay there, or get a strap to wrap around your neck—you'll want the glasses to be comfortable in any position if you need to take them on and off when running in and out of the sun.

Underwear: Wearing underwear while running is a matter of personal preference. Many runners forgo it altogether, especially if their shorts come with liners. However, it can add a layer of comfort under tights and unlined shorts. Cotton underwear may feel good when you start running, but once you begin sweating, it won't do you any favors, since cotton retains moisture. Instead, try a pair of the wicking underwear sold specifically for athletics in sporting goods stores: They should fit without binding and will keep you drier during your run.

Bra: A woman's running bra is a very personal choice and depends on body type. If you have smaller breasts, you may be able to get away with bras intended for low-impact sports such as rock-climbing. In fact, you may prefer these, since they feel less restrictive and bulky. If you have larger breasts, a bra designed specifically for the high-impact demands of running will provide greater support. You also may prefer a sports bra with a separate-cup design, rather than the more common sports-bra support system that holds the breasts in one compartment.

All women should look for wicking fabric, smooth seams that don't chafe, straps that don't bind around the chest and shoulder blades or ride up into the armpits, and a construction that allows for ease of removal; some bras are difficult to remove once they're damp with sweat. If you wear a backpack or hydration pack, make sure the bra straps still feel comfortable under the extra weight.

One last piece of advice: As I mentioned above, more and more products are marketed directly to trail runners—as opposed to road runners—so you can easily find attire clearly labeled for the trail. While some of these products have viable benefits—such as extra pockets or tougher material—others may be trying to cash in on the fashionable trail cachet with a "look." Whatever you buy, make sure the features make sense for the running you do, and don't fall prey to fads.

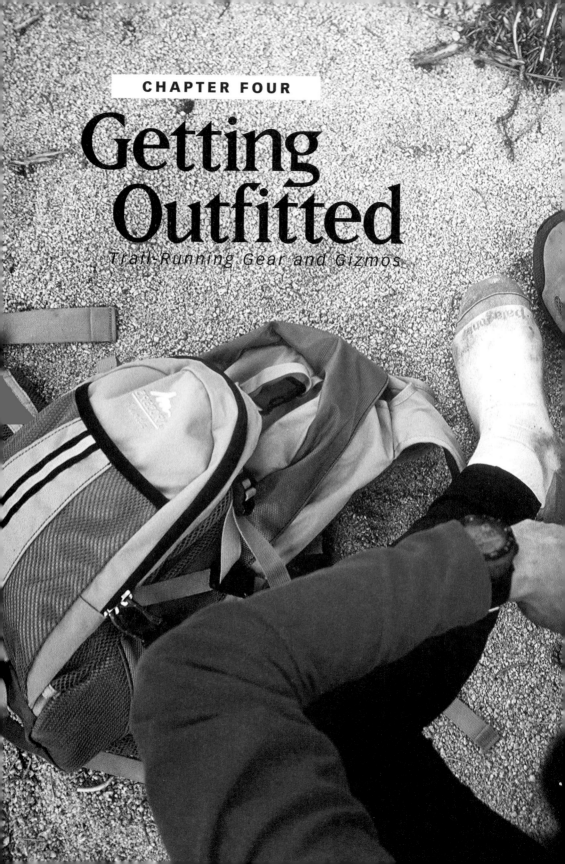

CHAPTER FOUR

Getting Outfitted

Trail-Running Gear and Gizmos

Runners, generally speaking, are a low-tech bunch. (If we loved gear, we'd be cyclists.) But trail running requires a certain pack-rat sensibility because, as with hiking, as soon as you decide to follow a trail away from civilization, you must remember to bring anything you might need while you're away. Of course, you can take this principle only so far, or else you'll be running with a 30-pound pack filled with a tent and food for a week—and you don't need me to tell you that you wouldn't be able to run very far with all that extra weight. My rule of thumb: Be prepared, not neurotic.

There's not a huge amount of gear actually marketed to trail runners. Most trail-running items fit under the heading of Things to Carry Other Things In. The most important item is a vessel for carrying water or sports drink, also known as a hydration system. This is the one piece of gear that virtually every trail runner should buy. Hydration systems are often combined with some sort of carrying pack for storing food and a handful of other items.

Just about all the other gear for trail runners is icing on the cake—if you've got some spare cash lying around, surely you'll find some nifty gadget to spend it on. That is, unless you've decided to take on ultramarathons, which open up a whole new world of gear you probably never knew about back when you were "just a runner."

Packs and Hydration Systems

Whether you're a minimalist looking for a tiny waist pack or a heavy traveler who wants a full-size backpack, it's worth the expense and trouble to find one designed specifically for running. (If you don't believe me, try wearing a conventional hiking pack and feel that thunk-thunk-thunking against your back with every step. You won't want to wear it a second time.)

Packs built for running have a flatter profile and construction that keep them close to your back, cutting down on excessive motion.

They're also exceedingly lightweight. Here are some other features to look for in a good running pack:

- Elastic cords or drawstrings that create a net on the outside of the pack so you can keep a piece of clothing within easy reach

- Lightweight mesh pockets that allow you to see what's in them and are great for stowing damp items

- At least one easy-access outside pocket for storing snacks that you can grab on the run without having to stop

- Comfortable padding in the back area and the shoulder straps

- A wide, contoured hipbelt

Some running packs span the full length of your back. Smaller versions are available, namely waist packs that sit on the lumbar region in the small of your back. Consider how long you run and how much food, water, and clothing you need to carry on your longest runs. Then try on several

A bottle-pack hydration system makes sharing bottles easier.

different models and ask the salesperson if you can take them for a test jog outside. Put some items inside the pack to mimic real-life conditions.

Other than shape and size, the most significant variables among packs are water-storage method and capacity. You basically have two choices: packs that hold traditional water bottles and packs that contain an internal reservoir for liquid.

Among bottle packs, you'll find designs for a single bottle centered in the small of the back, and designs intended to carry two bottles, one behind each hip. There are pros and cons to carrying good, old-fashioned water bottles. On the plus side, you can share bottles easily with others, and these packs are cheaper than the alternatives with built-in reservoirs. On the minus side, the weight and bulk of the water that's carried this way is more awkward than when it lies flat against your back. Also, you simply can't carry as much in a few bottles as you can in a pack with a larger reservoir.

If your long runs are all-day events, you'll eventually want to spring for a pack containing its own hydration

A tube leading out of the reservoir in a backpack hydration system allows you to drink on the go without any shifting, lifting, or other disruption to your running.

system. Packs with built-in hydration systems can contain larger amounts of liquid by storing it inside a waterproof reservoir built into the pack. The bladders in these packs are built to be very durable. "They're mostly rubber, so they last a long time," says Seattle-area trail runner and running-store owner Scott McCoubrey. "On occasion you might get a leaky bite valve, but all the manufacturers sell replacement parts." While early model reservoirs were tricky to keep clean, now they're constructed to allow easy access for scrubbing.

Holders and Holsters

If you don't want to be encumbered by a pack at all, you can find minimalist options such as bottle holders and holsters that hold just the necessities. Carrying a water bottle manually is infinitely easier with a hand strap that keeps the bottle in place with little effort from you. These cost just a few dollars, so you can try one out to see if you like it. Some runners prefer the convenience of having a bottle at the ready. The drawback is that you're always carrying something, a feeling other runners never quite get used to. A newer model waist strap holds several tiny bottles of water. On the plus side, these belts distribute the liquid's weight well and allow you to carry a variety of drinking options. The downside? They don't carry a whole lot.

You can also buy waist straps designed to hold a flask of sports gel and little more. Remember that you need to wash down that gel with water anyway, so it may be more efficient to purchase a small waist pack that holds your water bottle along with a few gel packets.

Water Purifiers

In areas with abundant natural water sources, you don't have to carry a whole day's worth of water on your back. Water purifiers allow you to take water from a stream and render it safe enough to drink.

Long a favorite water purification method of hikers, iodine wins points for simplicity. It's available in various forms, but tablets are the most easily portable. Iodine kills off most pathogens you'd likely encounter in a trailside water source, but it takes up to an hour to work. Here's a tip: Replenish your supply of water ahead of time. While you're drinking from one bottle, prepare another for your next use. Since iodine is notorious for its obnoxious taste, mix in a powdered sports drink to help disguise the flavor. (If you're running long enough to require purifying water, you'll want the added electrolytes anyway.) You can also purchase neutralizers that mask the iodine flavor somewhat.

In theory, portable water filters are an even better alternative to iodine. Backcountry filters once entailed lots of tubes, parts, and pumping, making them impractical for runners. Newer filters screw on to the top of a water bottle and filter the water as you squeeze it into your mouth. However, they "haven't fully evolved yet," says McCoubrey. "They're a little heavy and the water doesn't come through as easily as you might want it to." Therefore, most runners still prefer the iodine method.

Remember, the climate and terrain where you live and run will determine whether purification systems are feasible for you at all. "In the Cascades all summer there's lots of water," says McCoubrey. "You don't go more than 2 miles without hitting a stream or lake, so a hand bottle with a water treatment like iodine or a filter top gets you by." If you run in the New Mexico desert, obviously neither a filter nor iodine will do you much good.

Light Sources

Flashlights and headlamps obviously come into play when you're running in the dark, which, for the most part, means when you've entered the world of ultra running. The two primary light-source options are handheld types and those worn on your head. Many ultra runners carry both.

Lightweight flashlights will provide enough light for map reading or digging around in your pack, but they often end up held between your teeth when you need to free your hands. Larger, weightier flashlights can better illuminate the trail ahead of you. Headlamps provide good general lighting for the trail and will keep your hands free. While some run-

Navigational Tools

Most trail runners will never need to worry about bushwhacking their way through the unknown. It's trail running, after all—you're supposed to follow a marked path. Some more ambitious athletes will eventually find themselves in a situation—an adventure race, say, or a remote backcountry trail—where it's necessary to navigate. Or you might find yourself on an unplanned adventure, also known as getting lost. Anyone who spends time in the wilderness should learn to read a topographical map and use a compass, and should carry them when appropriate.

You may think that the whole map-and-compass thing is pathetically out of date now that you can simply purchase a Global Positioning System (GPS) receiver. Surely you've heard of these wondrous gadgets that tell you where you are, no matter where you are. Just press a button and you'll know the way, right? Well, not quite. Using GPS isn't as simple as tucking a receiver into your pack. You need fairly extensive training to use and interpret one properly; they work by tracking satellites to determine your position. "Many of the GPS units have built-in systems that point the way as you're moving. However, anything that's electronic—whether a digital compass or a GPS—is prone to failure," says Michael Hodgson, outdoor gear expert and author of *Compass and Map Navigator*. "So if you don't have a mechanical compass and map, then where are you?"

Where are you indeed? If you intend to buy a GPS receiver, Hodgson recommends signing up for a training clinic. To find out more about navigation in general, your local outdoors store can recommend classes or survival schools that cover GPS, compass, and map skills.

ners find a headlamp sufficient, carrying both a handheld and a head-lamp gives you a backup and also allows you to direct a brighter light on items the headlamp doesn't illuminate brightly enough, such as questionable rocks or roots.

When choosing a lamp, look for a secure head strap, possibly one that goes over the top as well as around your head. The lighter the device and the more stable its position on your head, the less it will bounce around. Bouncing is bad not only because it feels physically uncomfortable, but also because your light beam will bob disconcertingly down the path. Some headlamps come with options that allow you to

tip of the trail

Calling Out

A mobile phone isn't necessarily a bad thing to bring on a long run, but you never know if it will actually work when you need it. If you're heading into remote country for long periods of time, satellite mobile phones are an option. They work in many areas where conventional wireless service is not available, but they do require an unobstructed line to the sky. If you're in a forest, you still may find yourself unable to connect. Buying a satellite phone is a pretty pricey way to check in with your spouse. But you can rent one and have the option of trying to make an emergency call to civilization if you get lost or injured.

You may find a lower-tech tool handy if you get lost closer to your own backyard; try the old-fashioned whistle. It's cheap, doesn't take up much space, and weighs next to nothing. And while its range is clearly limited, it doesn't rely on complex technology to function.

strap them to your wrist (for greater control over the light's beam) or your waist (these are nice for getting the weight off your head).

A halogen bulb provides the brightest light and penetrates the farthest ahead on the trail, but LED lamps tend to burn longer. Consider running with a halogen headlamp and a spare battery for the best light penetration on the trail, and also carrying a small, handheld LED light as a backup. Bear in mind that the faster you run, the more light you'll need in front of you because you're looking farther ahead on the trail to plan your footfalls. Some lamps come with variable brightness settings, a useful option.

Gaiters

Lightweight and inexpensive, gaiters are a smart addition to your collection of trail-running gear. These short waterproof or waterresistant leggings cover the ankle and lower leg area and fasten to the tops of your shoes with elastic, Velcro, or laces. Gaiters offer protection from dirt, sand, gravel, and snow.

Trekking Poles

More often used by hikers, trekking poles are designed to help hikers maintain balance and absorb some of the shock of the trail. Trail runners sometimes rely on poles when ascending or descending

Gaiters are effective in either cold and mucky or dry and sandy conditions.

steep terrain with a heavy pack (most likely on a multiple-day outing). The poles work by providing additional points of contact with the ground,

Trekking poles help
keep you upright
when gravity works
against you.

thus distributing your weight and giving your legs a break. Trail-running purists say they would never run with poles, and many trail races ban their use. If you choose to run with poles, look for a model that can collapse down and fit into your pack. And when you do use them, be conscious of where you swing them: You don't want to trip up your neighbor.

Winter Running Gear

Crampons: Crampons are cleated devices that strap on to the bottoms of your shoes. They are a lightweight way to increase traction in icy or snowy conditions. They won't be comfortable once you hit dry ground, so be prepared to put them on and take them off (many times over, perhaps) if you encounter mixed conditions.

Warming packs: These are lightweight, disposable pouches made to hold in your hands or pockets. A chemical reaction creates heat when the pouches, which are filled with powdered iron and oxidizers, are opened and exposed to air.

Wintry conditions are no match for shoes fitted with crampons.

They provide a moderate heat source for hours and are a cheap, convenient backup in case your gloves don't cut it in the cold.

Snowshoes: When the snow gets too deep to run in, you can still run in it—in snowshoes. Snowshoeing is a terrific workout, one that will enable you to stay fit all winter if you live in a cold climate. When choosing snowshoes, look for a pair designed specifically for running. These will be smaller and lighter in weight than traditional snowshoes.

Snowshoeing is a great cardiovascular and strength workout.

They'll also have a narrower profile that tapers at the heel so you don't kick yourself in the leg with each step. Ask a salesperson to help you choose the right pair, since the size and weight of your snowshoe should relate to your own size and weight.

Running snowshoes also have bindings that are compatible with lightweight boots or shoes, and claws on the bottom that increase traction when you're pushing off. Expect to pay a few hundred dollars, and expect to appreciate every penny spent—these are nothing like your grandpa's rawhide and wood snowshoes. You'll be amazed at how closely your run in the snow can feel like regular running when you're armed with the right snowshoes. (For more on snowshoeing, see the cross-training information in chapter 10.)

CHAPTER FIVE

Trail Technique

Beyond Left, Right, Left, Right . . .

For flatlanders who've never run on anything steeper than a highway overpass, picking their feet up to get over rocks is the most intimidating thing about trail running. It's also one of the most difficult things to learn from a book. So I'll address technique here, to the degree that I can in print. But learning to negotiate your body over tricky terrain is a matter of practice, intuition, and training. Even when you've mastered those, you can still trip and fall hard. And you probably will.

That's important to understand and accept. "It's okay to fall. I fall a lot—it's not that big a deal," says Stephanie Ehret, a national-class trail and ultra runner. And she's in good company. Even the best trail runners often boast scraped knees and bruised shins. So don't think your goal should be to run stumble-free. A more realistic goal is to feel comfortable running and handling tricky situations.

Much of that comfort comes only with time and practice. I'm not talking only about physical practice. There's a huge mental component as well, since trail-running technique has a lot to do with confidence— the more you have, the better you'll run. It's similar to skiing: A nervous beginner will often lean back on her skis, feeling safer in a less aggressive stance. Ironically, she's more likely to fall in this posture, since she's shifting her center of gravity out of the optimal position. Once beginners gain enough confidence to lean farther forward, their likelihood of falling decreases.

The same idea is true of trail running. A timid runner may lean back on slippery downhill sections, for example, only to increase the chance that his feet will slide out from under him. The best approach on the trail is to relax and not succumb to fear. Don't spend so much time worrying about body position that you become flummoxed. Focus on the task at hand ("I want to land on that flat rock") instead of the negative possibilities ("I might fall"). Trail running is like driving a stick shift or working at a computer. Once you become familiar with the motions, your body moves automatically without your being conscious of your brain's instructions: "Right arm out. Left foot down."

Ehret puts it this way: "It's all about becoming comfortable and relaxed in your body. When you're relaxed, the more energy efficient and supple you become in your movements, and that's what makes a great trail runner. It's natural. Your body knows what to do; let it do what it needs to do. I'm not a very naturally graceful and proficient trail runner—if I can do this, anyone can. It's about getting out there and doing it and finding what works for you."

It may be more natural for Ehret than for some of us. She grew up in Colorado and hiked, climbed, and ran her way through childhood in the surrounding Rocky Mountain foothills. The movements she describes may not feel natural to someone who grew up in, say, downtown Cleveland. But that doesn't mean there's no hope for urbanites and their less-coordinated ilk. With practice, your body can learn these reactions and improve its sense of balance. It just takes time. Here are a few tips to get you started.

Focusing on the Trail

When you're unaccustomed to the uneven surface of a trail, it's natural to want to look closely at the placement of every footstep. But the more proficient a runner you become, and the more you pick up speed, the more you'll want to develop your ability to look ahead on the trail, rather than looking straight down at your feet. Your body needs time to react properly to upcoming obstacles, and if you look down at every step, it will react too slowly, and you'll stumble.

Not only should you look farther ahead, but you should learn to look directly at the clear line you wish to run. "Look where you want to go, not where you don't," Ehret says. "If you don't want to hit that big rock, don't look at it." The skiing analogy applies here, too, and if you've ever ridden a bicycle, you know it works the same way: When you want to avoid a bump while skiing or cycling, avoid looking at the bump. If you do look at it, you'll steer directly toward it. No matter how hard you may think, "Don't hit that bump," your eyes have the final say.

Softly scan the terrain a few steps down the trail for the best place to land. And pay attention. It's easy to get distracted by a compelling view or the color of a leaf on the ground. Don't get so casual and relaxed that you start admiring the redheaded woodpecker on that nearby pine while you're negotiating a rock-strewn slope. "Keep your head up and eye on the trail," Ehret says. It's easy to get lost in thought. "I'm the queen of spacing out on the trail," she says, and she has the war wounds to prove it.

Sometimes it's not so much a tendency to space out but sheer exhaustion that creeps up on you. It doesn't take much mental energy to run on a clear trail, but negotiating every step on a rocky trail for a long duration requires a tremendous amount of focus. If you begin to stumble or land on rocks you didn't intend to, it's a sign you need a mental breather, even if you're not huffing and puffing. Take a break and walk for a bit until you regain your focus.

Running Downhill

When you get good at running downhill, it's easy to fall in love with the feel of speed, the dance of placing your feet and knowing where you'll land. A gradual slope without too many obstacles is a great place to learn. You can practice looking ahead and placing your feet at a faster pace without feeling out of control. Save the steep descents for when you have a bit more experience under your belt.

"Running downhill is definitely more frightening on a trail than a road," says Brian Metzler, founding editor of *Trail Runner* magazine. "Your speed can get out of hand quickly. On a road with a smooth surface it's not the same issue, because you can slow down with good traction. But on a trail with scree or gravel, it can get scary."

This is where looking ahead on the trail is of primary importance, because as you gain speed, you'll have to react that much more quickly.

Make sure not to
overstride when
running downhill.

How to Fall

If you run on trails, sooner or later you're going to fall. It's not just the beginners who go bottoms up: Sometimes confidence can lead to cockiness, which has led to spills aplenty. And sometimes a fall is the result of nothing more than an unfortunate millisecond of miscalculation. "I just caught a toe and went down—the angles were all wrong," says Renee Despres of a small tumble with disproportionately large consequences. Despres put her arm out to break her fall and broke her wrist instead. "I never thought I could break a bone while running," she says.

Despres, an expert trail runner and a wilderness emergency medical technician, is no novice—and she's living proof that freak falls can happen even to the best runners. Luckily, she was less than a mile from the trailhead and was able to get help quickly, although it was a painful walk back.

"Falling is an art form," says Adam Chase, president of the All American Trail Running Association. Chase recommends practicing falls—on a soft surface, of course, and bundled in plenty of cushy clothes. "You need to learn how to roll, not brace yourself with your wrists, and cover your head in a big fall," he says.

The best way to fall is to use the reliable tuck-and-roll technique. That

means that instead of reacting by sticking out a hand to stop your fall, you should tuck your chin and arms to your chest and roll at impact, ideally taking a glancing hit on your side. Chase explains that by doing so, you maximize the surface area that makes contact with the ground, rather than absorbing the shock with one specific area—such as your wrist. "Also look at the ground and aim your fall, speeding it up or delaying it if you have to," he says. Try to decide in your split second of preparation whether a roll or bounce might help you. Despres points out that it's usually best to go with the fall rather than fight it. "Sometimes it's better to fall than to try to save yourself," she says. "You can wrench your back pretty badly fighting a fall."

Gloves can help protect your hands and give you confidence to put them down on rough ground if you do have to use them to stop your fall. Some trail runners prefer cycling gloves, which have padded palms and are light and airy. Long-sleeve shirts and longer shorts provide a layer of protection for your skin.

Of course, the best way to fall is not to fall at all, which requires more proficient running technique. "Avoid falling by really preparing for every step," Chase recommends.

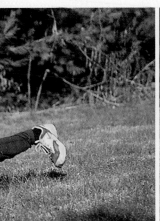

Shortening your stride can help you keep from gaining momentum too rapidly. Also, hold your arms and hands out from your body and up a bit to help your balance; this will also prepare your hands to brace you in the event of a fall.

Runners commonly increase the length of their stride as they pick up speed, but on the trail it's important to keep your stride in check. The longer your stride the faster you'll gain momentum. That's fine on a good surface with traction, but you'll zip along at your own peril on loose footing. An overextended stride can also wreak havoc on your knees. You'll place excess stress on your joints, causing severe soreness later that day—or later that decade. Keep your knees and feet under your center of gravity for maximal balance and joint health.

If you do find yourself going too fast for comfort, slow down by shortening your stride. If there's no solid footing around, consider running off the path—where you might find grass or solid rock rather than gravel—for just a few steps to brake yourself, the way a truck driver would use a runaway-truck ramp on a hilly highway.

Running Uphill

Running uphill may be more physically demanding, but it's a lot less scary than running downhill. So don't complain about your screaming glutes and pounding heart. This is the easy part.

"Easy?" you ask as you curse your way up a relentless climb. Yes, it is—as far as technique is concerned. That's because when you're running uphill, you go so slowly that you're always in control of where you land. In fact, you may go so slowly that you may as well walk. What's so scary about that?

"The key to running uphill is to shorten your stride and change the expectation," says Metzler. "Don't put so much pressure on yourself to run the same pace as on even ground. It's difficult to maintain."

Maintain good posture on uphill stretches.

Impossible to maintain is more like it. Your job when running uphill is to recognize when you've reached the point of diminishing returns. "Everyone will tell you it's smart to walk the uphills," Metzler says. "It's more energy efficient even if you're just on a run of 6 to 8 miles. It's better to slow to a walk than to waste energy."

So once you hit an uphill stretch of any significant duration, slow your pace and shorten your stride. As you decrease your pace, let your eyes focus a little closer to your feet. You still need to watch your step, especially if the terrain is rocky, but it's not as important to look ahead since you're moving slowly enough to react to the piece of trail that's right in front of you. If your breath becomes so labored and your heart rate so fast that you slow down dramatically, save your energy and walk. Once you catch your breath, pick up your jogging pace again.

A word about breath: It's very easy to allow your tired body to crouch over and crumple forward at the waist while you slog away at that hill. You should fight this very natural reaction to fatigue, since it's more important than ever to retain an upright posture on the hills. Bending at the waist doesn't allow your respiratory pathway to work efficiently. "It's hard enough to breathe going uphill, so you really need to try to open those breathing passages," says Ehret, who's also a massage therapist primarily for athletes. So concentrate on good, tall posture. You may have heard it's good technique to lean into the hills, and that's true. But lean from your ankles while keeping your body upright; don't lean or slump from your waist.

Handling Bumps in the Road

Roots, rocks, loose gravel, and mud are a fact of life in trail running. And sometimes they'll appear when you least expect them. Trails that are packed and smooth most of the year can turn into a muddy quagmire come spring. Some trails that are placid at the bottom morph into veritable jungle gyms as you approach the summit. Always be prepared and keep your eye on the trail—you never can be sure what you're going to get next. Here's how to handle most bumps in the road.

Rocks and roots: To clear these obstacles, adjust your stride by lifting your feet over them. A tiny root can be your downfall if you don't give it the space it needs. "I've had my trauma injuries from not clearing roots," says Douglas Wisoff, an age-group-champion ultra runner. "You have to make that transition quickly when you see them." In his case, three broken ribs and a month of no running resulted from his failure to make that transition quickly enough.

It can get tiring to run with an exaggerated leg-lifting motion, so pace yourself on prolonged sections of obstacles. If your legs get too tired to lift properly, slow down and walk the section rather than risk injury.

Scree: This accumulation of loose rock or gravel on a slope is the bane of most beginners. "Running on scree uphill is hard; downhill it's scary," Wisoff says. His trick for running on scree is to maintain a low center of gravity. "If I've

Trail Etiquette

Sharing the Trail

When the trail gets narrow, be polite about passing other runners—and about being passed. Wait until the trail is wide enough to pass someone comfortably. It's a good idea to call out which side you'll be passing on, as in, "On your left!" Likewise, always be considerate of those coming up behind you. If you hear someone closing in, look ahead for a wide-enough stretch of trail, then slow down and pull over to let him pass.

Remember, you'll be sharing the trail with nonrunners as well. Hikers (and possibly their dogs), mountain bikers, and horseback riders will all be proceeding at different paces. While larger and faster entities (bikes and horses) generally are supposed to yield to slower, smaller ones (like you), don't stake your skin on this principle. Always run defensively, and slow down and pull to the side when a bike or a horse approaches.

been carrying my arms up high for balance, I'll drop them a little lower. Also, if it's real steep and I'm in danger of gaining too much momentum, I'll do shorter steps with not so much braking action on the knees." While you don't want to lean too far back (remember our skiing analogy), you may want to adjust your stride so you're not leaning forward as much as usual. A gentle touch is key; braking hard on scree will have the opposite effect of what you intended and will send you into a nasty slide.

Mud: On the trail there's good mud and there's bad mud. Good mud just gets you dirty. Bad mud is the thick, sticky stuff that holds on to your shoes, glomming on until each foot weighs about 10 pounds more than when you started. Once you've collected half the trail on your outsole, there's no remedy except to sit down and clean off your shoes with a stick or leaves as best you can, and then try to avoid the worst patches.

Don't go off trail and break new ground on a dry patch just to save yourself some inconvenience, especially in environmentally sensitive areas. When it's muddy, the trail is already eroding. Detouring onto a fresh surface will damage the nearby ground and will only enlarge the patches of erosion.

Breathing

Breathing is generally natural and unconscious, but for runners it can pay to tune in to that simplest of functions. Ultra runner Ehret uses her breathing to gauge the effort the rest of her body is making. "Just being aware of it can be very relaxing, especially when pushing hard up a hill. Sometimes just listening to it does slow me down and relax things." That makes sense, because ragged breathing is an indication that you're heading into a zone of anaerobic effort that's not efficient for optimal running. By consciously keeping your breathing relaxed and even, you can help keep the rest of your body from tightening up and wasting precious energy.

Most runners take comfort in a rhythmic breathing pattern. Smooth, even breathing indicates to us that things are under control. When breathing gets ragged, too fast and hard, it may signal trouble. Especially at high altitudes, when you enter a state of oxygen debt—literally the point when you're not taking in enough oxygen to meet the demands of your energy output—it can be difficult to get out of. This is a bigger problem at altitude because the air is thinner and there is less oxygen to be had.

Relaxed, controlled breathing is not as easy to attain on a trail, particularly a hilly one, as it is on pavement. "On a track, my breathing coincides with my feet," says Metzler, who used to run primarily on the road and track on now runs mostly on trails. "But because you don't have any kind of consistent foot placement on a trail, it is difficult to have any consistent breathing." Not to worry, he says. You shouldn't expect a controlled breathing pattern on the trail. "For someone with a road-running background, it will feel awkward at first—you'll feel sluggish. But eventually you won't notice it. Give your body time to catch up, power hike up the hill, for example, instead of pushing too hard."

As a rule, stay in the aerobic zone on your trail runs. That means remaining in a zone of effort in which your muscles are able to get enough oxygen to operate efficiently—you'll know you're in the right place when you can talk somewhat comfortably during your run. When you shift to anaerobic training, you're no longer able to supply enough oxygen to meet your muscles' demand—a state of exertion you won't be able to maintain for long. You'll know you're at this point when you're out of breath and you can feel the accumulation of lactic acid in your legs, which has a deadening effect. This is something a sprinter or middle-distance runner would do; a trail runner concentrating on longer distances doesn't need to achieve that kind of exertion.

When Running Becomes Climbing

If you run in mountainous, technical areas, you're bound to face stretches where running becomes more like climbing. When you're faced with an unfamiliar climbing situation, take baby steps: Climb up a few steps, then come back down. Then go up a few more steps, and repeat the process.

Some trail runners become so focused on forging ahead during a run that later they find they've scaled something they can't get down. "It's incredible how much of a mental thing that is instead of physical,"

Facing Fear

I'm well aware that there are some people who would get a good laugh out of the idea of my writing a chapter on trail-running technique. I'm not exactly the most coordinated athlete, which is one of the reasons running appealed to me early on. On one backpacking trip with friends—friends far more skilled than I at such outdoors techniques as water purifying, tent staking . . . *walking*—we all went on a trail run one afternoon. I was going along just fine until we came to a stream crossing. Mind you, this wasn't a river crossing. It was a pretty little babbling thing about as wide as I am tall, and conveniently littered with a few stepping-stones. The water was cold, however, perhaps a foot and a half deep, and moving fast.

I froze up. It wasn't a fear of drowning, obviously. It was a seemingly irrational, idiotic fear of getting my feet soaked. No matter how I tried, I couldn't get myself to cross. While my friends skipped quickly across and waited for me with mounting impa-

says Adam Chase, president of the All American Trail Running Association. "You can get up pretty high and then realize your anxiety, and it's almost a paralysis. Once you lose it big-time you're really stuck, like a cat up a tree." If you've never done any formal rock-climbing, take a tip from the pros and "downclimb" in proper form: facing the rock surface. You'll have superior control and maneuverability when you face the rock and grip with your hands. If you keep your back to the rock surface, you'll have less balance and control.

Whatever your experience level, stay focused and true to your own abilities. If you ever get to a point in climbing where you feel uncomfortable, call it a day and turn around.

tience and looks of incredulity on their faces, I stood paralyzed.

What my partners didn't know was that I was afraid of facing the rest of the trip with wet feet because I suffer from Raynaud's disease, which, for me, is a mostly inconvenient but not dangerous circulatory disorder that cuts off the blood supply in extremities when they're exposed to even slight cold. Wearing wet socks overnight could mean frozen, white toes in the morning. Still, I could only blame so much of this on old Raynaud. In the end, it was my focus on the possible negative outcomes that kept me from crossing the water. My friends finally and understandably grew tired of waiting and started moving down the trail. That was probably a favor to me, since it jump-started a worse fear—that of being lost and alone, which clearly outranked the fear of having wet feet— and it spurred me into action. I crossed the stream with a few minor splashes to my toes, but no big deal, and I was off. It was much ado about nothing, and it was all in my head.

I wish I could say that experience cured me of all such fears, but I still have irrational moments when I'm faced with critical points on the trail. My inner chicken refuses to surrender that easily.

CHAPTER SIX

How to Train

Taking Your Workout to the Trail

Trail-running workouts follow the same principles as road or track workouts, with some adaptations. Training on trails lends itself to what the running world calls long, slow distance, or "LSD"—long runs of comfortable pace that can also be interspersed with walking. Because of surface and terrain changes, speed and cadence become secondary considerations on the trail.

If you're a road runner, you're more accustomed to measured workouts of a specific distance or at a specific pace, so trail training may take some adjustment. As I mentioned in chapter 2, the main adjustment you'll want to make is to your mindset. It's difficult to equate a trail run with a run you'd do on the roads. You can't have expectations about regular pacing because of terrain changes, so you'll need to relax and switch the focus from your watch to your overall effort. "A 6-mile loop on a trail is such a different sensory experience than a 6-mile loop on the roads," says Brian Metzler, founding editor of *Trail Runner* magazine. "The biggest tradeoff is that on the roads you can go faster, but on the trail more strength is involved."

Plenty of trail runners don't consider what they do "training." And it's perfectly fine—arguably running at its best and simplest—to run for as long as you like, as fast or slow as you like, as much as you like, and never to give a thought to formal training concerns. Plenty of trail runners, particularly those with little interest in racing, take this relaxed approach and never worry about keeping a running log or varying their workouts. More structured training comes into play for runners who want to increase speed, particularly for racing, or those who come from a road-racing background and want to combine road and trail running. For these runners, it is possible to maintain more structured training even on the unstructured environment of trails. In the rest of this chapter we'll talk about the variety of training that's possible on the trail.

Leaving Mile Markers Behind

For almost all trail runs and all types of workouts on the trail, it makes sense to measure your runs by time, not distance. This means your goal and end result will be marked by an amount of time, such as 1 hour of running, rather than a number of miles. There are several reasons for this, but the most obvious one is that most trails are not measured or particularly measurable. Beyond that, the footing, elevation gain, and surface condition mean that it's often not appropriate to attempt to stick to a consistent pace. And it's certainly not helpful to compare your pace on one trail of a specific length to your pace on another different type of trail. Your time and effort on two trails of the same length can vary greatly. So plan your workouts in terms of hours or minutes spent running. That's also how you'll want to record the end result in your training log, if you keep one.

Mixing Road and Trail

Many runners who enjoy trail running will still do some running on roads for any number of reasons, including the available terrain where they live and their time and work constraints. Both types of running work perfectly well together and are, in fact, quite complementary.

Runners who train seriously and like to race on the roads can still benefit from trail running. The trail provides a great strength workout, one that's especially beneficial early in the season or during the base-building phase of running. During this period, the focus is solely on slow mileage to increase a base of endurance and aerobic conditioning, which the runner can later build on to increase speed. Even professional road racers mix trail running into their workouts. They know that what they give up in speed on a particular run, they will more than make up for in strength building.

If you plan to race on roads, train at least once or twice a week on pavement. If you only run on the softer surfaces of trails, your legs won't become "road tough." Training on a harder surface is not something you want to do every day, because it's a leading cause of stress fractures in runners and tends to be harsh on joints. But that same strain on a limited basis will, in fact, toughen up your bones and connective tissues. That's necessary preparation, especially if you intend to run a long race—such as a half-marathon or longer—on the roads. Metzler tells this cautionary tale of one acquaintance who trained for the San Diego Marathon only on trails. On race day, he felt a sharp pain in his midsection by 10 miles and was forced to drop out at the halfway point. He was later shocked to learn that he had a hairline pelvic fracture, probably because his body was unaccustomed to the impact of running on a hard surface.

Mixing Workouts and the Trail

Trail workouts can be as much play as work. Hilly courses in particular lend themselves to the type of running you probably did as a child: charging uphill, going fast, and then slow, waiting for the rest of the gang behind you, and then breathlessly gathering speed all the way to the bottom. It's fun and games—and great training, too.

The idea behind most workouts is to mix periods of faster work with recovery periods, thus training your body aerobically to handle faster paces for longer periods of time. Such workouts also build strength by forcing your legs into a faster turnover and making them run harder on hills. They're ideal if you plan to race shorter distances— a 5-K up to a half-marathon. Even if you're training for races of marathon distance or longer, adding one faster workout a week or mixing it into a longer, slower run can build spring into your step that you wouldn't otherwise develop. The added strength will keep your legs from getting stale from repeated slow runs.

Workouts to Try on the Trail

Here are some simple—and fun—ways to increase your strength and liven up your workout routine.

Fartlek: A Swedish term that means "speed play," fartlek is ideally suited to trail runs. Fartlek workouts can be as stringent or loose as you care to make them. They generally consist of running segments that alternate faster, up-tempo stretches with slower recovery stretches. You can run according to your watch or landmarks. If you use your watch, alternate intervals of anywhere from 15 seconds to a minute. For example, jog for 15 seconds, then run faster for 15 seconds, then jog for 15 seconds, and so forth. If you use landmarks, employ the same principle, picking out spots ahead of time to shift gears: at the top of the hill, for example, or at the upcoming tree.

When doing fartlek workouts, the goal is to complete the run without stopping. Think of the faster segments as shifting one gear higher, not as all-out sprinting—you don't want to put yourself in oxygen debt. Likewise, keep your recovery segments at a jogging pace; avoid walking or stopping. Warm up well with a few miles of easy running before beginning your fartlek running.

Tempo runs: Typically, tempo runs are a predetermined distance of several miles run at a faster pace than an everyday run. The point of a tempo run is to get you used to running faster for longer distances. A tempo run is a good workout to do early in the race season and as you approach competition time.

Road runners do tempo runs at a specific pace based on their 10-K pace and level of aerobic fitness. A trail tempo run likely won't allow you to measure distance accurately, and your pace will be approximate at best. That's fine: A tempo run need not be precisely engineered for it to still be beneficial.

Runners who race distances up to marathon length can especially benefit from the speed building of the tempo run. Kevin Setnes, one of the nation's premier ultramarathon coaches, likes tempo runs for racers of even the longest distances. "Ultra runners are guilty of becoming very good slow runners," he says. "I like to have people work on their speed. Weekend to weekend, they go longer but go at a very slow pace, so during the week I have them do a lot of tempo runs."

To do a tempo run on a trail, find a stretch of several miles with good, even footing. Rolling hills are fine, but you don't want to do a tempo run on a technical trail or one with severe elevation changes.

tip of the trail

How Hard Is Hard?

A word about workouts: One of the most common mistakes runners make as they become more serious about training is to run their workouts too hard. Workouts should be quality efforts, but never as hard as a race effort. Some coaches have been known to describe it this way: There's race energy, and there's workout energy. If you use your race energy in your workouts, it won't be there for you when you're ready to race.

So train hard, but train smart. Don't destroy yourself trying to keep up with training partners who are too fast for you, or trying to set a new speed record for your workout each week. Save that type of energy for the real races.

Too much variation in the terrain makes any attempt at consistent pacing impossible. Warm up well, then do your tempo run at a pace you can consistently maintain for the duration of the segment. This should not be an all-out effort that leaves you completely expended. You should feel as if you could complete another 5 minutes at the same pace if you had to. You can run for time—anywhere from 20 minutes to 1 hour—or for distance—typically 2 miles for a beginner to 8 miles for a more advanced marathon runner. If you're new to tempo runs, start with a shorter one and gradually build up the distance by adding 5 minutes a week.

Intervals: Typically, intervals are considered a track workout, and they're indeed beneficial for runners who want to know their precise pace based on a measured track. However, it is possible to run intervals on trails. Intervals build leg speed, which means they are important for races of shorter duration. Trail runners who are racing on the roads or doing shorter trail races should consider doing interval workouts once a week during racing season.

An interval workout consists of running repeats of a short, predetermined distance alternated with a resting interval. You can do trail intervals on a short loop, or out-and-back intervals on a short stretch of trail. This workout is different from a fartlek in that it consists of timed and measured segments that can be compared; it's different from a tempo run in that it is not a sustained effort.

You should conduct interval workouts at a fast pace—typically your 5-K road-racing pace or a little faster. The trick to this workout is not to go too hard: Complete the last repeat as fast as or faster than the first, but without getting so tired that you struggle to complete the workout. You generally should cover between 2 to 4 miles of total distance in the repeats, not including warming up and cooling down.

If you don't have a measured trail, run your interval workouts based on time. Mark off how far you run at a brisk pace for 1 minute, 2 minutes, and 3 minutes, for example. Then conduct your interval workout going back and forth between these markers, striving to consistently hit the same mark in the same amount of time. An example of a workout might be two sequences like this: 1 minute, 2 minutes, 3 minutes, 2 minutes, and then 1 minute, with rest between each repeat. Or for a more speed-oriented workout, try four repeats of 1 minute, then four repeats of 2 minutes, and then four repeats of 1 minute.

Hill work: Hill workouts are the ultimate strength builder. There's no way to become proficient—or even comfortable—running hills except to train on them. And if you plan to compete on hilly courses and don't practice on hills, you'll face a painful shock come race day.

The simplest hill workout is to run a hilly trail at your usual comfortable pace. Instead of taking it easy on the hills like you would normally do, try to push up them, resting or slowing down once you've reached the top. You can also do more formalized hill repeats, which entail running hard up a hill then jogging back down several times. When doing hill repeats, keep the duration of the hill from 30 to 90 seconds; any longer than this, and you'll be going too slowly for the benefits you're seeking from this workout. If the hill takes you longer than 90 seconds, just turn around wherever you are at that point and head back down the hill.

Some runners like to practice running hard downhill, which is good training for your legs because it engages different muscles than running uphill and develops fast leg turnover. It can also strain your knees if you overdo it. Go only as fast as you can while maintaining control, and keep your stride length in check so you don't jar your knees with too much braking action on the landing.

The easy run: Runners of all abilities should do easy runs all year long. The purpose of the easy run in your workout mix is to let your body recover from more difficult efforts, while still logging some miles to build and maintain fitness. Beginning runners will do most of their running at an easy pace as they gain fitness and adapt to the stresses of running. More serious runners will want to do easy runs in the base-building phase (to build aerobic endurance) and in the harder training phases (to recover between more challenging workouts). Runners who stick to the trail exclusively will want to do much of their running at an easy to moderate level.

The trickiest part of an easy run is keeping it easy enough. Slow doesn't always mean easy. A run on a very technical trail or one with severe elevation changes can be very slow but not count at all as an easy day, as your legs will surely let you know when you're finished. Lots of climbing will leave you feeling like you've just completed a weight workout, and in a way, you have.

When you want to run easy, choose a trail with flat terrain or rolling hills. Look for a trail with comfortable footing and few obstacles, allowing you to relax and exert minimal effort. Easy runs generally are not the time to explore: Be familiar enough with the trail so your easy run doesn't turn into an all-day odyssey.

The pace of an easy run will vary from runner to runner, but the effort for each individual runner should remain consistent. The best way to monitor your effort is with your breathing: You should be able to carry on a conversation with a training partner. If you're too winded to talk, slow down or walk until you recover.

Your easy runs may vary from day to day. Runs that are equal in pace and distance can feel different from day to day depending on how tired you are from previous workouts. Douglas Wisoff, who has won his age group three times in the prestigious Leadville 100-Mile Trail Race, points out that on some days, an easy 10-mile run can "feel like I didn't even run." Other days, he says, it's a much more grueling proposition. So be prepared to change your running plans—slow your pace even more or cut short the duration—to ensure that your easy day doesn't turn into a tough workout.

Heart-rate monitors may be a good way to gauge your effort, depending on the terrain you're running. Many runners who use a heart-rate monitor prefer them for the specific purpose of keeping their easy runs slow enough to truly stay in a recovery zone. In general, the flatter the trail, the more accurate and helpful a monitor will be. (For more on training with a heart-rate monitor, see "The Heart-Rate Monitor Debate," on page 78.)

The long run: The long-run workout is perfectly suited to the trail. A typical training schedule contains one long run per week, generally on the weekend, when it's easier for you to find time and training partners. And partners are more important for runs of this length than any other. They make it easier to focus because someone is either helping you maintain the pace over a long period of time or distracting you with conversation. Running partners are also nice to have around in case of complications, which increase in likelihood the longer you're out on the trail.

The duration of your long run depends on your training background. Beginners might consider anything longer than an hour to be a long run. Serious trail runners, and ultra runners in particular, often spend the better part of a day on their long runs, logging upward of 30 miles. The key to the long run is to build up gradually—you obviously don't get to that point overnight.

If you're already an experienced road runner, adapt your long runs to the trail based on the time you spend running, not the distance you usually cover. In other words, if you typically go 11 miles in 90 minutes, plan to run for 90 minutes on the trail, or even 5 to 10 minutes shorter until you get comfortable with the new terrain. You may cover a shorter distance than what you normally do, but your effort will be greater and you may find yourself walking through more challenging portions.

Once you're comfortable on the trail, you can increase the duration of your long run. A general rule of thumb: Increase the run by roughly 10 percent from one week to the next. Once you run comfortably on the trail for 90 minutes, bump it up to 100 minutes.

How long does your long run need to get? That depends on your goal and your personal preferences. If you run for fitness alone, you really don't need to run for more than 90 minutes. Plus, hydration and fuel concerns become more complicated once your run exceeds this length of time.

However, most trail runners get bitten by the long-run bug and eventually extend their runs farther and farther. Training for races of marathon distance and longer will require a long run of at least 2 to 3 hours or more.

Some trail runners determine run length based on how they feel on a given day; others just go as far as their training group goes. That's fine, but don't talk yourself into something you're not prepared for. Run with partners who are close to your level of experience or who at least are willing to accommodate your needs.

It's fine to walk on your long run. In fact, that's the only way you'll be able to stay out there long enough if you're training for a race of marathon distance or beyond. Speed should not be your consideration for these workouts. The benefit of the long run comes from the

The Heart-Rate Monitor Debate

Wouldn't it be great if you had a device that could tell you exactly how hard you should run each day for optimal fitness? It could beep at you when you needed to speed up or slow down. It could ensure that your rest days stayed easy and tell you if you were really working hard enough on your quality training days.

Some people believe such a device already exists: the heart-rate monitor. This training tool uses electrodes (in a strap you wear around your chest) to transmit your heart's signal to a watchlike device worn on your wrist. Most monitors allow you to set target heart-rate zones for your workouts, and some get so fancy that they do practically everything except run for you.

Some trail runners swear by their heart-rate monitors. Bob Rayburn, a trail runner based in Colorado, says his runs have improved vastly since he's strapped on a monitor. "Different trail conditions will inspire you to run harder than you want or make you think you're going faster than you really are. So without the monitor, it's like driving a vehicle without a tachometer—you don't really know your efficiency," he says.

The monitor also helps remind him to maintain the effort he intended for that day's training. "For years I've gone out saying, 'Today's going to be an easy run,' but then I start out and find myself saying, 'I feel good,' and it becomes a tempo run." The monitor keeps reality in check. And it helps him stay consistent during long runs. "In the past I'd go out for 30 miles, and after 22 or 23 miles I'd do a lot of walking just to get it over. Now I use the heart-rate monitor to keep it very slow at the beginning, and on the hills crank it way back [making it easier]. At the end I can run the whole 30 miles rather than walking part of it."

The monitor even has its place in racing. "It helps me to run *my* race," he says. "During trail races it's so tempting to keep somebody else's pace. You get talking with a few other runners, you're going their pace, and before you know it your heart rate rises. You get wrapped up in the excitement of things and stop running *your* race. Sensibly, with a monitor, you break off the conversation and let the heart rate come down."

So why doesn't everybody use one? For one thing, there's some question about the accuracy of the information they provide. Every runner has his own maximum heart-rate and training-efficiency zones, and determining those numbers is complicated. Formulas abound, along with controversy about which is best. Many variables enter the mix, including age, gender, altitude, and hills. It's not as easy as punching in a few numbers and magically knowing how fast you should be running.

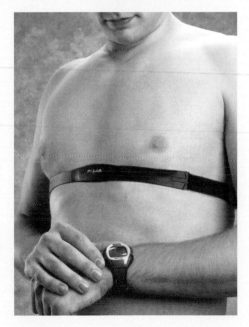

Also, many runners enjoy running because it affords them a sense of freedom. They simply don't like to be attached to a gadget and prefer to run based on feel, even if how they feel leads them into a less-than-optimal workout. This feeling may be even stronger among trail runners—Luddites that we are—than other runners.

TRAIL MIX

The Long Run, and Then Some

My husband, Arturo Barrios, is a professional runner who eventually turned to coaching after his retirement from competition. He mostly coaches national-class runners—conventional road racers, not trail runners. However, his athletes run on trails several times a week as part of their training, both for the altitude benefits and the strength work from the variety of hills.

One day a group of about 10 of his athletes headed out for what was supposed to be a roughly 12-mile loop in the foothills southwest of Boulder, Colorado. As the run went on, the guys naturally broke into a few smaller groups based on their pace. After a little more than an hour, one small group returned to the trailhead, then another, but after 90 minutes or so, it became clear that a few runners were missing. Another 20 minutes went by. People began to get concerned. Another 20 minutes passed. Some of the runners got in their cars or trucks to search the connecting roads. Cell phones were dialed.

After 3 full hours the missing runners reappeared, straggling wearily down the mountain. Their original run should have taken an hour and 20 minutes. It turns out that after running together for a while, they had stopped when one runner had to tie a shoe. They lost sight of the rest of the group, then disagreed about the route, and tried what they thought was a shortcut to catch up. Some shortcut. This was one long run that turned out to be much longer than planned. The moral of the story? Think twice before trying new paths you've never taken when you're doing a planned workout. Oh, and make sure you double-knot your shoelaces before you start running.

time spent on your feet. Go as slowly as you need to in order to be comfortable.

Remember to bring along supplies for the journey. The bare minimum: some type of sports drink and a food source. Runs longer than a few hours will likely necessitate a fanny pack with the addition of a first-aid kit, an extra clothing layer, and of course, more snacks. Quick carbohydrates with some sugar and salt are a good bet, and lay off the heavy fiber.

CHAPTER SEVEN

Trail Racing

Preparation and Training

Many runners shun formal competition for all sorts of reasons. Some don't think they're fast enough to race. Others have nasty memories of coming in last at some high school sporting event. Some purists even believe that racing somehow sullies the true essence of running—they say they don't need the affirmation of measurement that races provide.

But racing is about far more than measurement and testing yourself against others. It's about testing yourself against *yourself*. And it's meant to be fun. So if you're the type of runner who shies away from the starting gun, you may want to reconsider.

Running races are the rare athletic competition where the very best participate in the same contest as the very slowest. Cycling, for example, divides competitors into categories for races. And can you imagine a football game where you and your buddies played in the same game as the pros? When you run a footrace, the pressure is off from the get-go. Let's face it: Except for a handful of elite runners, most of the competitors certainly are not racing to win.

If you know you're not going to win, why race? Here's why:

- To test yourself
- To see how far you've come since last year
- To see friends and have a good time
- To meet new runners and share an experience
- To try new things
- To have a goal for your training
- To feel as if you've accomplished something special
- And, yes, for some, to see how fast you can go

Trail races are usually even more low-key than road races. By the very nature of the ground they cover, trail races are more about the experience than about measuring success. It's impossible to compare your time from one course to another—routes vary greatly in hilliness, altitude, and surface conditions—so the times you run are of dubious significance. Often the terrain itself is the star of the show, and the runners who participate count themselves lucky to share a run in a beautiful or challenging place.

Of course, many runners take trail racing very seriously. And if you want to test yourself against others, you'll find no shortage of opportunities. But racing is for everyone. And if you've never tried it, you're missing a very special, rewarding aspect of the sport.

Choosing and Scheduling Races

To find events in your region, look for flyers at your local running store. For races farther afield, check out race calendars in running magazines and on Web sites. Then, map out a race calendar for yourself at the start of the running season or the beginning of the year. This will give you a target, help you organize your training, and if necessary, motivate you to make travel plans. First, choose one or two races to highlight and concentrate on; these will become the focus of your training. Many runners like to pick a race of substantial distance—a marathon or an ultramarathon —or a race at a beautiful destination to plan a vacation around.

Once you've chosen your highlight races, find some smaller races to round out your schedule. For these secondary events, look for competitions closer to home so that they're easily accessible. And choose shorter, easier competitions that will help you tune up for the big ones.

For best results, once you're in shape, try planning a race about every third weekend in the competitive season, which is typically the summer and autumn in most parts of the country. Some race lovers will schedule a race for every weekend or even twice a weekend—once on Saturday and once on Sunday. While this is fine if you love racing, it probably won't result in the fastest race times. If you're constantly racing, it's harder to train properly because you're always in recovery mode or resting for upcoming races. On the other end of the spectrum, if you race less than once a month, you won't benefit from the practice that comes from testing yourself in competition. You may feel stale, awkward, or mentally unprepared when you finally do enter a race.

Sample Racing Schedule

The races leading up to your goal race should work as tune-ups so you can see where you stand in your training. If your goal race is longer than a half-marathon, your earlier races should stay on the shorter side, so you don't drain too much of your energy. A summer race schedule leading up to a 15-mile trail race might look something like this:

WEEK 1: no race

WEEK 2: no race

WEEK 3: 5-mile road or trail race

WEEK 4: no race

WEEK 5: no race

WEEK 6: 10-mile trail race

WEEK 7: no race

WEEK 8: no race

WEEK 9: no race

WEEK 10: 5-mile road or trail race

WEEK 11: no race

WEEK 12: 15-mile goal race

When choosing races for your calendar, the most important factor to consider is the distance of the event. The race that's the focal point of your season should be a distance that you're confident you can train for in the time you have. Allow 4 to 6 months to train for a marathon or ultramarathon, and about 3 months to prepare for distances like the 10-K or half-marathon. You can be ready for shorter distances—2 to 5 miles—in as little as 8 to 10 weeks, providing that you've already built a base with endurance runs of up to an hour.

In addition to distance, also consider the type of course: whether it's hilly or flat, at altitude or not. If you train in a relatively flat area, it's probably not wise to run a race with lots of hills. And if you're unable to train at altitude, you probably don't want to suffer through a race at high elevation.

Your race calendar will provide a framework around which to build your training for the best possible racing results. It needn't be written in stone. If you find out about a race partway through your

tip of the trail

Don't Get Shut Out

Some trail races can accommodate only a limited number of entries. The reasons vary: Maybe the event is being held on environmentally sensitive land, or the logistics of the course require a lot of workers and volunteers for each runner. As a result, some races grant entry on a first come, first served basis; others require qualifying times; and still others hold a lottery. Find out far ahead of the race date if the race you want has a predetermined cutoff for entries and how to enter, then follow the rules closely for your best chance at entry.

season and want to run it, you can always switch things around to fit it in and compensate.

Preparing for a Trail Race

Once you've chosen a race, get as much information about the course as possible. The course information will encourage you to tailor your training to the event by, say, running practice hills or traveling to a similar altitude for your training runs. The idea is to simulate in your training the conditions you'll encounter on race day. Request route and elevation maps from race organizers as soon as you've entered. Sometimes this information is included with the race entry form, but other times it's not offered unless you ask.

If you live near the race location, try to run the course beforehand. You'll learn which parts are easy or difficult, and you can strategize about where you'll want to push yourself or take it easy during the race. If the course is too long to run all at once, break it up into segments, covering different pieces on different days by driving to access points.

Also, run course-specific workouts to train for the rigors of individual races. For example, if you know the race finishes uphill, plan some workouts in which you run hills near the end, when your legs are tired. Likewise, it's just as important to train your legs for the downhills to acclimate them to the pounding. Many runners mistakenly discount downhill stretches as easy, and therefore fail to prepare for them. In fact, prolonged downhills in a long race can take a severe toll on quadriceps and knees.

Other smart race preparations include:

Talk to people who have done the race before. They can offer such insider information as where the footing gets tricky, where competitors speed up or slow down, or where things get bottlenecked on a narrow stretch.

Check the weather report. Many races keep statistics on race-day temperature and conditions. This will help you plan what to wear and carry. Prepare for surprises. Weather can be unpredictable in many parts of the country where trail races are held.

Find out what provisions aid stations will offer. Most races will tell you ahead of time what to expect at aid stations. Longer races will provide food and drink during the race. If the food or drink is not what you've been training with, carry some of your own during the race.

Try out all your equipment and clothing before the race. When you're racing, you want to be familiar with all your gear so that it doesn't pose any problems for you. This is most critical when it comes to shoes. Be sure you have the right pair of shoes for the terrain you'll be racing on, and take care of this detail weeks ahead of race day. If you've worn out the pair you've been training in, don't wait until the last minute to buy a new pair. Give yourself several weeks to try a new pair so you can be sure they

Trail Etiquette

Buddy System

Training with a partner or group is a wonderful way to stay motivated and ensure that you'll do the required work every day—as long as you share the same goals and schedules. If your partner wants to do a hard workout and it's supposed to be your easy day, or if she wants to run only for an hour and you're scheduled for longer, you've got to be able to bow out gracefully. Some runners avoid such scheduling conflicts by training with partners only on easy days, so there's complete agreement that the runs are supposed to be recovery efforts and nobody will be tempted to push the pace. Others will get together only on harder workout days, agreeing in advance what the training will be. Whatever strategy you take, stay true to your own needs, and go it alone when necessary. If you become too much of a team player in running, you risk injury, burnout, or even slacking off.

don't cause blisters or hot spots on your feet. Ditto if you need to buy a new pair of shoes for a rocky, hilly, or sandy course: Always give yourself several runs before race day to make sure the shoes work for you.

Race-Training Schedules

One of the reasons people appreciate running on trails is because it requires less structure than road running, with its measured miles and times. And even when it comes to racing, trail runners tend to be more free-form about their training programs than other runners.

Stephanie Ehret, one of the top female ultramarathon racers in the country, eschews a predetermined workout schedule. "My husband [record-setting ultra runner Peter Bakwin] is very scientific in his training—he could tell you exactly how many miles he does and when he does hills and speed. That approach doesn't work as well for me," Ehret says. She describes the planning that goes into her typical training week this way: "When I feel great, I run fast; when I don't, I run slow. When I have a good week, I put in a lot of miles. I do a lot of long slow distance. But I do fartlek, too. At the end of the run, I'll always push. Oh, and sometimes I try to get a 'free' speed workout: I run fast downhill—getting leg rhythm up without the effort."

This type of training might be relaxed and unscheduled, but that doesn't mean it's haphazard. Ehret listens very carefully to her body, which is a good lesson for any trail runner. Whether you follow a formal schedule or wing it each day, pay attention to the signals your body sends in the form of energy or attitude, sleepiness or hunger. Only you can know how tired or fresh your body is at any point in a run. Only you can know if you're putting in too few or too many miles. "You have to know who you are," Ehret says. "It's more intuitive than anything."

It's intuitive, yes, but it's also scientific. Every runner will benefit from following certain basic training principles, which generally involve the physiological laws of work and recovery. To gain fitness from the work you do, you must allow your body periods of recovery. Otherwise you'll stress your body repeatedly, tearing down muscles and eroding your immune system instead of gradually building them up. You can't outrun the laws of nature, so mix easy days of slow, short runs into your training.

The Laws of Rest

The principle of rest and recovery works both in the short term and long term. After a hard day of running, plan an easy day or take a day off. Likewise, after a hard season of racing and training, take it easy for a few weeks, or take them off entirely. This principle applies no matter how fast or slow you are or how long you've been running.

The rest-and-recovery concept should be a no-brainer. But that is not so for many runners, who are notorious for their addiction to the sport. If 10 miles are good, then 15 are better. If running once a day becomes easy, why not try twice? The problem is that runners don't always recognize—or heed—the signs of overtraining. Early symptoms include lethargy, lack of energy on runs, difficulty sleeping, and mood swings. Ironically, if you're addicted to running and your performance suffers, you may think the answer to your sluggish state is to run harder and faster. In reality, you need a break.

Overtraining is an insidious affliction that can eventually compromise the immune system, leading to lingering colds or injuries. To avoid overtraining, pay attention to what your body tells you. This is particularly true when you follow a formal training schedule, which you may feel obligated to adhere to—to the letter. No single training program works for everyone. Any training program, no matter how good, can be adjusted so that it's more realistic for you. And when you feel your body could use a break, be sure to take one. You'll come back stronger and more energized for your next workout.

Training for a 5-K to Half-Marathon

The training schedule below is designed for intermediate runners. Beginners can decrease the overall mileage and change one of

5-K to Half-Marathon Training Schedule

	WEEK 1	WEEK 2	WEEK 3	WEEK 4
MONDAY	45-min easy distance	45-min easy distance	45-min easy distance	45-min easy distance
TUESDAY	20-min warmup, 15–20-min fartlek, 20-min cooldown	20-min warmup, hill workout of 10 × 1-min hills, 20-min cooldown	20-min warmup, interval workout (4 sets of 2 min hard, 2 min easy jog, then 1 min hard and 1 min jogging), 20-min cooldown	20-min warmup, 20-min fartlek, 20-min cooldown
WEDNESDAY	60-min easy distance	60-min easy distance	60-min easy distance	60-min easy distance
THURSDAY	Off or cross-train	Off or cross-train	Off or cross-train	Off or cross-train
FRIDAY	20-min warmup, 3-mi or 20-min tempo run, 20-min cooldown	20-min warmup, 4-mi or 25–30-min tempo run, 20-min cooldown	20-min warmup, 3-mi or 20-min tempo run, 20-min cooldown	30-min easy plus a few strides at up-tempo pace for 80–100 meters
SATURDAY	45–60-min easy distance	45–60-min easy distance	45–60-min easy distance	20–30-min easy
SUNDAY	90-min long run	100-min long run	100–110-min long run	**RACE** (5-K to half-marathon)

the quality workout days (Tuesday and Friday) to an easy distance day. Advanced runners can increase both the easy distance and the workout distances. The schedule represents the month leading up to a key race; it assumes the runner has already built a comfortable base of distance with runs of 45 to 60 minutes five times a week. This particular training schedule lends itself well to runners who divide their training and racing between trail and road—you can do the workouts on either surface. (As I mentioned in chapter 6, if you plan to race on roads, run at least one workout a week on a hard surface to train your legs.) You'll notice that this training schedule features short intervals to build speed, tempo runs for strength, and long runs that are not excessive, so you don't lose valuable leg speed.

Because the terrain of trail races can vary to a great degree, consider the topography of the races you'll be running, as well as the distance. If you'll be racing on hills, run some of your workouts on longer hills. If you'll be dealing with descents, the same idea applies. If you plan on running numerous races during a season, choose one or two to focus on more seriously and gear your training toward these. You can't peak for every race, so think of the smaller races along the way as training for the high-priority ones.

This schedule will work as a solid introduction to training for a shorter race, such as a 5-K or 10-K. If you use this schedule to run a longer race, such as a 10-miler or half-marathon, you may want to allow for a few more weeks of training. Simply repeat week 3 once or twice, increasing Sunday's long run to up to 2 hours.

Training for the Marathon

Marathon training requires a buildup phase of anywhere from 4 to 6 months. The most important workout when training for the marathon is the long run. Skimp on these runs, and you won't make it through the race. You can be more flexible with your other runs during the week and can do more or fewer speed-based workouts, depending on your racing goals. A good rule of thumb is that speed work—any-

Training for the Marathon

	WEEK 1	WEEK 2	WEEK 3	WEEK 4
MONDAY	45-min easy distance	45-min easy distance	45-min easy distance	45-min easy distance
TUESDAY	20-min warmup, 15–20-min fartlek, 20-min cooldown	20-min warmup, 20-min hill workout (repeats or just a hilly course), 20-min cooldown	20-min warmup, 25-min fartlek, 20-min cooldown	20-min warmup, 30-min fartlek, 20-min cooldown
WEDNESDAY	60-min easy distance	60-min easy distance	60-min easy distance	60-min easy distance
THURSDAY	Off or cross-train	Off or cross-train	Off or cross-train	Off or cross-train
FRIDAY	20-min warmup, 3-mi or 20-min tempo run, 20-min cooldown	20-min warmup, 4-mi or 20–25-min tempo run, 20-min cooldown	20-min warmup, 30-min hill workout, 20-min cooldown	45-min easy distance
SATURDAY	45–60-min easy distance	45–60-min easy distance	45–60-min easy distance	30-min easy
SUNDAY	90-min long run	100-min long run	110-min long run	**RACE** (10-K or similar distance)

thing faster than your regular pace, including intervals, hills, and tempo runs—should account for no more than 10 to 15 percent of your weekly mileage. So if you run about 60 miles a week, you could cover about 2 miles in an interval session and another 4 to 5 miles in a tempo

	WEEK 5	WEEK 6	WEEK 7	WEEK 8
MONDAY	45-min easy distance	45-min easy distance	45-min easy distance	45-min easy distance
TUESDAY	20-min warmup, 30-min fartlek, 20-min cooldown	20-min warmup, 30-min hill workout, 20-min cooldown	20-min warmup, 30-min fartlek, 20-min cooldown	20-min warmup, 30-min fartlek, 20-min cooldown
WEDNESDAY	60-min easy distance	60-min easy distance	60-min easy distance	60-min easy distance
THURSDAY	Off or cross-train	Off or cross-train	Off or cross-train	Off or cross-train
FRIDAY	20-min warmup, 4-mi or 25–30-min tempo run, 20-min cooldown	20-min warmup, 5-mi or 35-min tempo run, 20-min cooldown	20-min warmup, 30-min hill workout, 20-min cooldown	20-min warmup, 6-mi or 45-min tempo run, 20-min cooldown
SATURDAY	45–60-min easy distance	45–60-min easy distance	45–60-min easy distance	45–60-min easy distance
SUNDAY	120-min long run	135-min long run	150-min long run	90-min long run

(continued)

Training for the Marathon—cont.

	WEEK 9	WEEK 10	WEEK 11	WEEK 12
MONDAY	45-min easy distance	45-min easy distance	45-min easy distance	45-min easy distance
TUESDAY	20-min warmup, 15–20-min fartlek, 20-min cooldown	20-min warmup, 20-min hill workout, 20-min cooldown	20-min warmup, 30-min fartlek, 20-min cooldown	20-min warmup, 30-min fartlek, 20-min cooldown
WEDNESDAY	60-min easy distance	60-min easy distance	60-min easy distance	50-min easy distance
THURSDAY	Off or cross-train	Off or cross-train	Off or cross-train	Off or cross-train
FRIDAY	20-min warmup, 3-mi or 20-min tempo run, 20-min cooldown	20-min warmup, 4-mi or 25–30-min tempo run, 20-min cooldown	20-min warmup, 3-mi or 20-min tempo run, 20-min cooldown	30-min easy distance, plus a few strides at up-tempo pace for about 100 meters
SATURDAY	45–60-min easy distance	45–60-min easy distance	45–60-min easy distance	30-min easy
SUNDAY	180-min long run	195-min long run	210-min long run	**RACE** (Half-marathon or similar)

run. Or if you run 9 hours a week, you could run a 45-minute tempo run and do another 25 minutes of faster running in interval or fartlek workouts.

This schedule will take you through the last 4 months of training before the race. (It assumes that you can run for an hour several times a

	WEEK 13	WEEK 14	WEEK 15	WEEK 16
MONDAY	45-min easy distance	45-min easy distance	45-min easy distance	45-min easy distance
TUESDAY	20-min warmup, 15–20-min fartlek, 20-min cooldown	20-min warmup, 30-min hill workout, 20-min cooldown	20-min warmup, 20-min fartlek, 20-min cooldown	20-min warmup, 15-min fartlek, 20-min cooldown
WEDNESDAY	60-min easy distance	60-min easy distance	60-min easy distance	45-min easy distance
THURSDAY	Off or cross-train	Off or cross-train	Off or cross-train	Off or cross-train
FRIDAY	20-min warmup, 4-mi or 25–30-min tempo run, 20-min cooldown	20-min warmup, 5-mi or 35-min tempo run, 20-min cooldown	20-min warmup, 3-mi or 20-min tempo run, 20-min cooldown	30-min easy distance, plus a few strides
SATURDAY	45–60-min easy distance	45–60-min easy distance	30–45-min easy distance	20–30-min easy
SUNDAY	180-min long run	120-min long run	60–80-min long run	**RACE** (Marathon)

week and can complete a 90-minute long run.) I've built some races into this schedule because they're a good way of testing your fitness and developing the mental preparation required for competition. The schedule includes some easy days before each race to give your legs a break from the intense training.

CHAPTER EIGHT

Race-Day Strategies

Maximizing Your Potential

Race day is payoff day—the time when all your hard work is rewarded. And that doesn't apply just to speedsters. No matter what your pace or finishing position, a race is the icing on the cake. The following tactics will help make the icing taste that much sweeter.

The Night before the Race

Prepare for the race as much as possible the night before. The last thing you want to worry about on race day is running around the house trying to find four safety pins to affix your number to your shirt. Many runners find comfort in having a routine for the night before the race. They'll eat the same meal, set out their race clothes, and go to bed at a preset time. It may sound a little obsessive, but it serves a purpose. For one thing, a routine minimizes the chance of mishaps, such as suffering from an upset stomach or forgetting your racing shoes. Just as important, a routine can keep jittery nerves calm, focusing your attention on something other than the race itself.

Here are the basics to include in your prerace routine:

Eat a high-carb, low-fat meal that's familiar. This is not the time to experiment with new foods that can wreak havoc the next morning. Go easy on fiber and fat, since they can cause digestive distress later on race day. Many runners prefer the traditional pasta dinner the night before the race. This is a great choice because it's high in carbohydrates. It's also a winner because it's a safe bet in most restaurants: You're unlikely to get sick from a plate of spaghetti. You can make it even safer for your stomach by omitting the tomato sauce.

Have a beer if you want. Especially if you think it will relax you or help you sleep. Stick to just one. Drink any more and you may still feel the effects of the alcohol early on race morning.

Have sex if you want. Runners fall into two camps on this issue: Some believe abstinence the night before a race helps conserve precious energy. Others believe the benefits of relaxation help them sleep. It's your call. You can rest comfortably either way knowing that nobody's ever proved that prerace sex hinders performance.

Set out all your race clothes and paraphernalia. Pack your race bag with everything you'll need: shoes, socks, hat, sunblock, water bottle, energy bars, jacket, race directions, wallet, and whatever else you'd like to bring. Pin your number to your race shirt now so you won't lose it in the morning.

Set two alarms if you can. You'll rest better knowing that at least one of them will go off. And if you're away from home, don't rely only on hotel staff for a wake-up call—they often forget. Set the clock radio on your bedside table as a backup. But check the time first, because hotel clocks are notorious for being inaccurate.

Go to bed at your usual time. If you go to bed much earlier than usual, chances are you won't get more sleep. Instead you risk lying in bed fretting over the race. Turn in at your usual time and try to relax. And don't worry if you can't sleep. One night of tossing and turning won't actually harm your performance. It's far more important to be generally well rested—that means getting enough sleep during the full week before the race. Then if you have a bad night's sleep the night before the race, your reserve tank is full.

Race Strategy

No matter how fast or slow you run, a race-day game plan will make the experience that much more rewarding. If you know ahead of time how you intend to run, you can avoid classic racing mistakes such as starting off too fast or expending all your energy on hills. Once you have a plan, stick with it. Many runners waste all their preparation and hard work when they abandon their strategy and follow another racer who runs too fast or too slow. If you don't remember the phrase "run

Warming Up for the Race

The point of a warmup is to prepare your body for the rigors of running hard in a race. You're not a race car: Your body is not designed to go from zero to full throttle in just a few seconds. That means before you toe the starting line, you'll want your heart rate to be just slightly elevated and your muscles to be limber.

The longer the race, the less of a warmup you need. That's because your pace will be slow enough in long races (marathons and ultramarathons) that you can essentially warm up during the race. For those races, it's more important to conserve energy than to expend it by warming up.

For shorter races, a proper warmup can ensure that you'll run up to your potential and can lessen the likelihood of an injury—such as a pulled muscle—that can result from sudden exertion.

Here's a step-by-step warmup plan that takes 30 to 40 minutes:

▲ Jog very slowly for about 15 minutes—just 5 minutes or so for marathons

▲ Stretch thoroughly for 10 minutes

▲ Use the toilet one last time, if necessary

▲ Change into racing shoes or racing clothes if they're different from what you're wearing

▲ Do a few strides—not sprints, just regular strides, right around your race pace—of about 50 meters (omit this step for the marathon and longer races)

▲ Get into place at the starting line and continue to jog, walk, and stretch while you wait for the race to begin

your own race" from earlier in this book, commit it to memory right now—it's a wise strategy for all runners.

While you should definitely run the pace that's right for you, some racing rules apply to everyone. Stick to them and you'll run your best race possible.

Run Consistently

You have only so much energy and you want it to last for the whole race. Surging quickly and then backing off will tire you more rapidly than maintaining a consistent effort. It's better to find a level of effort you can maintain for the duration of the contest.

In trail races, effort is more important than pace. In a flat road race, runners strive to run exactly the same times for each mile of the race. This is virtually impossible in many trail races. So pay more attention to your effort and try to keep your pace as consistent as possible within the variety of terrain you'll cover. Let's take a closer look at that idea: When you run uphill, of course you slow down. But you want to try to crest that hill with reasonable energy expenditure—without draining all the energy from your legs, resting much, or walking so slowly that you hardly move.

Trail Etiquette

Starting Lineup

In any race, it's important to position yourself appropriately at the starting line. The speedsters should be up front, with slower runners bringing up the rear. The reason for this is obviously so that the slower runners don't interfere with or get trampled by the faster runners, who get off to a quick start. This is doubly important in trail races, which can narrow to a single-file passage early in a race. You certainly don't want to force the faster runners to go around you or get stuck behind you on a narrow stretch. If you're not sure where to position yourself, ask runners around you how fast they plan to run to get an idea where you should start.

For most runners, that means covering a long, tough hill at a slow, steady jog or a brisk walk. Once you top the hill, you'll pick up your pace, but the effort will feel about the same because you're on easier terrain.

The better you know yourself as a runner, the more accurately you can gauge your effort. That's where training comes in: The longer you've been running, the better you'll be able to plan your races. If you're new to racing, be conservative when estimating how hard and fast you can run.

Start the Race Conservatively

It's much easier to come on strong in the later stages of a race if you start at an easy pace. If you start off too fast, you may come to an abrupt halt when you surpass your aerobic limits (you may need to walk or jog to the finish). Runners call this "hitting the wall," or "bonking." Whatever you call it, the end result is always the same: No matter how hard you try or how much you want to run faster, your legs won't let you.

Find a Pacing Partner

During the race, find someone who's running at your pace, and stick together. Instead of considering this person a competitor, think of him as a motivating force—you're working together to keep going. But always remain conscious of how you feel during your race. It's great to run with others as long as they help you maintain the right pace for you. If your pacing partner speeds up or slows down to the point where you're no longer running the right race for you, find another runner to team up with.

Maintain Your Concentration

Your race success depends on your ability to stay focused. In training it's okay to zone out now and then to admire the wildflowers along the way. (And if you're not trying to maximize your effort, it's fine during a race, too.) But when your mind wanders, you slow down. To maintain concentration keep a constant monologue going in your head, reminding yourself, "Stay relaxed. Maintain your pace. Keep it up."

Training with a partner is good preparation for running a race with a pacing partner.

Don't Panic If You Don't Feel Great

In many races, especially longer ones, you'll go through microcycles of feeling good and feeling not so good. If you start to feel tired or just generally crummy, wait it out. After a while you'll cycle into feeling better. By remaining calm and mentally strong, you'll increase the likelihood of recovering physically during the race.

Plan a Strong Finish

Races always feel more satisfying when you finish with a surge of speed rather than a grim march. In fact, ending with a fast spurt, or "kick," is typical strategy for shorter races. Many novice runners take this too literally, hoarding all their energy and then rallying in the last few meters when they'd be better off using more of that energy earlier in the race.

In trail racing a more gradual acceleration of pace in the last 400 to 800 meters is ideal. I'm not suggesting an outright sprint; rather, a slight increase from the intensity of the pace at which you ran the balance of the race.

One of the best ways to ensure a strong finishing kick is to plan where you're going to turn it on beforehand. If the configuration of the course allows, check out the last half-mile of the course while you're warming up. Then choose a landmark about a half-mile or 600 meters before the finish line. When you pass this landmark in the actual race, this will be your reminder to pick up the pace. This mental strategy works wonders when you're worn out and approaching the finish: If you've already planned to give it your all at that point, you'll probably find an extra reserve and try that much harder. Without this preplanned marker, you'd just muddle your way to the finish line.

In races of longer duration—anything longer than 6 to 10 miles—there's not much point in saving for a finishing kick. The goal in these races is to finish at your race pace and not slow down significantly. If you can run a half-marathon or marathon in which you managed to finish at about the same pace you started, you ran a smart, strong race.

After the Race

The race is over. Hopefully you ran well. Maybe you didn't run as well as you thought you could. Either way, something good can come out of it.

If you succeeded in running your goal time or completing a distance you'd never run before, then your training is on track. Keep a record in your log of how you felt during the race, what you think worked in your training, and what you did right mentally along the way. Build on this success by maintaining the type of training you've been doing or slowly enhancing it.

And if you didn't run as well as you wanted to, don't despair. Use the opportunity to learn some lessons. Ask yourself where you felt weak in the race. Did you lack strength on the hills? Did you not have enough speed in a short race or have trouble keeping food down in a longer one? The best runners use every race as a learning experience, tweaking their training and making changes so they improve the next time around. By asking yourself, "What can I learn from this?" you focus on the positive. This not only helps you train for the next race, but it also keeps the racing experience fun.

Also recognize that some days you just don't have it. You might have done everything right in your training but still run a disappointing race. Maybe things have been stressful at home or at work. Maybe you didn't taper your training enough in the week before the race—or maybe you tapered it too much—and you felt sluggish. Whatever the case, know that everybody can have a bad day. It's best just to shrug it off and try again next time.

Meanwhile, take care of business after the race by cooling down properly. A good cooldown will minimize muscle soreness and tightness and allow you to resume training more quickly. Jog very slowly for about 10 to 15 minutes. Do some gentle stretching. And eat and drink as soon as possible after the race to restore your energy.

CHAPTER NINE

Ultra Racing
Training and Tactics

Some people just can't get enough of trail running. For them there's the ultramarathon. The term refers to any distance beyond a traditional marathon. That can mean just slightly longer—say, a 50-K (roughly 31 miles)—or much, much longer. Fifty-milers, 100-milers, and 100-plus-milers are all out there for the conquering.

To the uninitiated, running a race several times longer than a marathon sounds crazy. But most ultra runners didn't start their running careers with a goal to run 100 miles. It's more that they couldn't stop once they started. "Once you get on trails, it's so nice you just keep running," says Douglas Wisoff, a champion masters ultra competitor. "It's meditative when you're out there that long."

Ultra running also tends to attract a more mature crowd: older, more patient, less focused on speed. It's a perfect fit for runners in their forties and fifties, whose fastest days are behind them but who still want to challenge themselves. "People's values change as they get older, and they're looking for something else with their running," says Wisoff. "It's a way to test your endurance as you get older. And 100 miles is kind of a milestone, isn't it?"

When you decide to tackle an ultra, it makes sense to ease into it with a "shorter" ultra. "The short-distance people who want to graduate to ultras should probably go through a marathon first, then a 50-K," says Kevin Setnes, an exercise physiologist and one of the premiere ultra-running coaches in the country. "The 50-K is a fairly short step from the marathon, but in some ways it's even easier, because you have the mentality that 'I can take my time, eat and drink, and maybe even walk a little bit.' When you say 'ultra distance,' people don't press as much as they would for 26.2 miles."

Champion ultra runner Peter Bakwin agrees these "intro" ultras can be less grueling than they might seem. "In some ways a 50-K or 50-

miler is easier on the body than running a road marathon," he says. "It's a lot slower, and you run with the idea of just completing the distance, not a personal record."

Training

The training approaches for a marathon and an ultramarathon are remarkably similar. The bottom line: Even though these races are of a tremendous duration, one can only train so much. Even for the best ultra runners, there comes a point of diminishing returns in terms of time spent training.

Training for ultramarathons isn't really about duplicating the race's duration—you can't. It's about readying your body physically and mentally for the challenge. That means becoming as fit as possible with the optimal amount of running, honing your eating-and-drinking-on-the-run technique, and preparing yourself psychologically for the intense mental focus required for an event of this nature. When you're training, you should try to duplicate race conditions as much as possible. This may mean doing some nighttime runs, during which you can get used to placing your feet in the dark and can test your headlamp.

Taste the Ultimate

Many longer races allow competitors to have pacers run alongside them. You can get a feeling for the ultra experience before committing to a race at all by volunteering to do this. Helping out as a pacer is a fun and easy introduction to the sport for you and it means company, emotional support, and assistance (carrying food and clothing) for the runner.

Also test different foods and drinks to see what agrees with you, and be sure the clothes and shoes you've chosen don't rub or chafe.

The training schedule here is based on recommendations from accomplished ultra runners and coaches. According to Setnes, the buildup period required for an ultra is the same as that for the marathon: 4 to 6 months. The key difference between ultra and marathon training is the duration of the long runs. Whereas a marathoner will eventually do a long run of 18 to 22 miles, the ultra runner who's training for a 50-miler will typically run for 4 to 8 hours on the trail, covering distances upward of 30 miles. It's during those very long runs that it's most important to re-create race conditions, in this case by walking uphill sections and running the downhill ones. You not only enable yourself to run longer, you'll train your walking muscles as well, and learn the type of pacing required for the race. This switch in thinking about the long run is critical: Unlike other races in which walking is anathema, in ultras, walking is requisite.

While plenty of ultra runners include those 30-mile-plus runs every weekend, Setnes doesn't recommend it. If you're logging high mileage every weekend, it becomes very difficult to work on the running speed that Setnes claims is important even for ultra runners. Instead, he recommends alternating long runs of up to 30 miles one weekend, with a quasi-long run of 15 miles the next weekend. That allows you to focus on more quality work during the week—tempo runs and even track workouts. This strategy is geared toward elite types who truly want to compete in an ultra, but it pays dividends for recreational runners as well.

Another benefit of alternating your long-run weeks is that it gives you an emotional break and lessens the likelihood of illness, injury, and burnout. Since it takes tremendous mental and physical energy to run 30 miles or more week after week, giving your body a break every other week means you're more likely to make it to the starting line of your planned race.

Some ultra runners also like to do back-to-back long runs on the weekends, teaching their bodies to "run tired" by running, say, 30 miles on Saturday and then 20 miles on Sunday. Setnes prefers to restrict the long run to Saturday, allowing two days (Sunday and Monday) to recover for the week of training ahead. "If the training involves some type of speed work on Tuesday, [you] are better off (and safer) taking two easier days of rest before getting into the midweek workouts, which are important," he says.

The schedule below assumes you have already built a significant base, are used to doing speed workouts already, and are able to complete a long run of 90 minutes' duration. Before attempting this training, ideally you should have trained for and completed a conventional marathon. The long runs in this schedule increase by far greater increments than in traditional marathon training; but you'll spend a greater amount of time walking on these long runs, making them less stressful on your body. This schedule also includes tempo runs and fartlek runs during the week. If you're a beginning ultra runner or are just feeling fatigued, you can adjust the schedule by turning one of those workouts into an easy distance run.

Ultra-Racing Strategies and Tactics

Running 100 miles really is a different sport than racing shorter distances. The ultramarathon is as much a contest of will and stubbornness as of physical endurance. "So much of it is mental—it's not just the fitness, it's the confidence to go out and do it," says Bakwin, who, with a friend, set the record for running the John Muir Trail in California, covering the 223 miles in just over $4\frac{1}{2}$ days.

You gain that type of confidence much the same way you gain fitness: through training. When you put in the long training hours required for a race of this length, you build a base of physical and mental strength. You experience the trials and doubts you'll inevitably face during the race—and knowing you've successfully negotiated these trials on training runs helps build the mental toughness you need for the race. When race day comes, you'll be able to think back on your training and feel confident that you did the required work.

Beyond mental toughness, racing in ultra marathons also requires you to focus on logistics. "As the distance gets longer, other things come into play—your eating strategy and pacing strategy," Bakwin says. In

Training for a 50-Miler

	WEEK 1	WEEK 2	WEEK 3	WEEK 4 (RECOVERY WEEK)
MONDAY	45–60-min easy distance	45–60-min easy distance	45–60-min easy distance	45–60-min easy distance
TUESDAY	20-min warmup, 15–20-min fartlek, 20-min cooldown	25-min warmup, 20-min hill workout, 25-min cooldown	25-min warmup, 30-min fartlek, 25-min cooldown	25-min warmup, 30-min fartlek, 25-min cooldown
WEDNESDAY	90-min easy distance	90-min easy distance	90-min easy distance	90-min easy distance
THURSDAY	20-min warmup, 3-mi or 20-min tempo run, 20-min cooldown	20-min warmup, 4-mi or 25–30-min tempo run, 20-min cooldown	25-min warmup, 30-min hill workout, 25-min cooldown	45-min easy distance
FRIDAY	Off or cross-train	Off or cross-train	Off or cross-train	Off or cross-train
SATURDAY	90-min long run	120-min long run	150-min long run	180-min long run
SUNDAY	45–60-min easy distance	45–60-min easy distance	45–60-min easy distance	Easy 45 min of running

short, the longer you're out running, the more things can go wrong. For example, if you wear the wrong clothes to race in a 10-K, you may get a little cold or hot. If you wear the wrong thing in an ultra, you'll have to drop out of the race.

Fueling for extreme endurance is typically the trickiest aspect of ultra running for beginners. Without experimenting, there's no way to know how your body will react to different food and drink. Even diligent preparation in training runs is sometimes no match for the real thing—novice ultra runners often take several stabs at a 100-mile race before figuring out how their bodies will respond and what they require.

	WEEK 5	WEEK 6	WEEK 7	WEEK 8
MONDAY	45–60-min easy distance	45–60-min easy distance	45–60-min easy distance	45–60-min easy distance
TUESDAY	25-min warmup, 30-min fartlek, 25-min cooldown	25-min warmup, 30-min hill workout, 25-min cooldown	25-min warmup, 30-min fartlek, 25-min cooldown	25-min warmup, 30-min fartlek, 25-min cooldown
WEDNESDAY	90-min easy distance	90-min easy distance	90-min easy distance	90-min easy distance
THURSDAY	25-min warmup, 4-mi or 25–30-min tempo run, 25-min cooldown	20-min warmup, 5-mi or 35-min tempo run, 20-min cooldown	25-min warmup, 30-min hill workout, 25-min cooldown	20-min warmup, 6-mi or 45-min tempo run, 20-min cooldown
FRIDAY	Off or cross-train	Off or cross-train	Off or cross-train	Off or cross-train
SATURDAY	210-min long run	150-min long run	240-min long run	150-min long run
SUNDAY	45–60-min easy distance	45–60-min easy distance	45–60-min easy distance	45–60-min easy distance

(continued)

Training for a 50-Miler—cont.

	WEEK 9	WEEK 10 (RECOVERY WEEK)	WEEK 11	WEEK 12
MONDAY	45–60-min easy distance	45–60-min easy distance	45–60-min easy distance	45–60-min easy distance
TUESDAY	25-min warmup, 30-min fartlek, 25-min cooldown	20-min warmup, 20-min fartlek, 20-min cooldown	25-min warmup, 15-min fartlek, 25-min cooldown	25-min warmup, 30-min hill workout, 25-min cooldown
WEDNESDAY	90-min easy distance	60-min easy distance	90-min easy distance	90-min easy distance
THURSDAY	25-min warmup, 3-mi or 20-min tempo run, 25-min cooldown	Off or cross-train	25-min warmup, 3-mi or 20-min tempo run, 25-min cooldown	20-min warmup, 6-mi or 45-min tempo run, 20-min cooldown
FRIDAY	Off or cross-train	45-min easy distance	Off or cross-train	Off or cross-train
SATURDAY	270–300-min long run	30-min easy	300–330-min long run (5 to 5.5 hours)	150–180-min long run
SUNDAY	45–60-min easy distance	RACE (Half-marathon or similar distance at "workout" intensity— not all-out effort)	45–60-min easy distance	45–60-min easy distance

It's crucial to begin drinking and eating early in the race to avoid a fuel or water deficit—even if you feel fine for the first few hours. During your prerace training, decide how many calories you want to consume each hour and set a schedule. Experiment on your training runs with different items. And talk to as many other ultra runners as possible and learn what works for them. (For more on fueling during ultra-marathons, see page 118.)

	WEEK 13	WEEK 14	WEEK 15	WEEK 16
MONDAY	45–60-min easy distance	45–60-min easy distance	45–60-min easy distance	45-min easy distance
TUESDAY	25-min warmup, 30-min fartlek, 25-min cooldown	25-min warmup, 30-min hill workout, 25-min cooldown	25-min warmup, 20-min fartlek, 25-min cooldown	20-min warmup, 10-min easy fartlek, 10-min cooldown
WEDNESDAY	90-min easy distance	90-min easy distance	60-min easy distance	45-min easy distance
THURSDAY	20-min warmup, 4-mi or 25–30-min tempo run, 20-min cooldown	25-min warmup, 4-mi or 25-min tempo run, 25-min cooldown	20-min warmup, 3-mi or 20-min tempo run, 20-min cooldown	30–40-min easy jog
FRIDAY	Off or cross-train	Off or cross-train	Off or cross-train	20-min easy jog
SATURDAY	330–360-min long run (5.5 to 6 hours)	180-min long run	90-min long run	Off
SUNDAY	45–60-min easy distance	45–60-min easy distance	45–60-min easy distance	**RACE** (50-miler)

"In the end it comes down to trial and error," Bakwin says. And a little bit of luck. "Just like great marathoners are blessed with high VO_2-max [a measure of the body's ability to utilize oxygen during exertion] and perfect form, the people who do really well at 100-milers are blessed with a great internal system. The rest of us, after a while, our system shuts down."

Pacing is the other critical yet tricky part of racing ultras. And just like fueling, all the training in the world won't prepare you for how you feel during a race. The words of wisdom remain the same from virtually everyone in the ultra world, however: Start off slower than you think you need to. You'll never hear someone finish an ultra saying, "I wish I'd gone out faster." Instead, the common lament is, "Why did I start off that fast?!"

For all but the best ultra runners, proper pacing also means knowing when to walk. In a 100-mile or even 50-mile race, walking virtually all the uphill sections and jogging the flat and downhill stretches is a smart strategy. You can use training runs to develop an efficient, rapid walk—you'll cover ground as quickly as if you were jogging, but you'll use less energy.

Finally, it may sound contradictory, but enjoy yourself out there. Ultras are all about the process. Just finishing one is the challenge—and the reward.

Fueling for Ultra Endurance Races

"Ultra runners are the healthiest athletes I know—because they have to be," says Alice Lindeman, Ph.D., R.D., a specialist in endurance nutrition. It doesn't take long for ultra runners to learn that if they don't take in adequate calories for their training, they'll pay the price: The question isn't whether they'll bonk, it's just where they'll be when it happens. "Everyone has their war stories," she says, "whether it's eating a mashed Twinkie off the side of the road or asking a farmer for some tomatoes from a field. I know people who have eaten field corn!" The point is that if you're going to run for hours on end, you've got to eat—a lot.

The fueling preparation for an ultra or a long training run should begin well before you start running, according to Lindeman. For an ultra race, you need to consume adequate overall calories, especially in carbohydrate form, for a full week before the race. For a long training run, prepare similarly for at least one day in advance. It's also important to begin limiting your fiber intake during this time period. "Start cutting back on the fiber, especially the soluble type, which produces gas when bacteria in the gut ferment it," Lindeman explains.

During a long run or race, the most important aspect of fueling is to maintain adequate carbohydrate intake to fuel your muscles with glycogen. This is one instance when it's worth doing some nutritional math: Your target is to consume 1 to 2 grams of carbohydrate per kilogram of body weight per hour of training or competition. (Multiply your weight in kilograms times 1 or 2. Then multiply that amount by the expected number of hours of your run.) You can carry your carbs in the form of foods—fruit, graham crackers, or bagels—or with sports drinks and liquid "meals," such as instant breakfast drinks. "You have to stay on schedule," Lindeman says. "Just like you have an idea of the pace you want to maintain when you run, you have to do the same thing with eating."

The other critical element during long runs and races is to stay hydrated. Lindeman recommends drinking early and often—starting a drinking regimen 20 minutes into the run and drinking every 20 minutes thereafter. Sports drinks are fine, as is water, so long as you supplement with food. Many runners like to alternate between plain water and a sports drink. (To learn about the dangers of drinking just water on long runs, see the sidebar on page 155.) Gauge whether you're drinking enough by monitoring your urination. "Just because you're sweating, that's not enough," Lindeman says. "You have to be drinking enough to pee."

Practice eating and drinking during training runs. You never want to be stuck experimenting with new foods and fuels during an ultra race. If you're traveling to a race and are not certain what stores or restaurants are in the area, bring your own food and drink. (For more on nutrition for running, see chapter 11.)

CHAPTER TEN

Beyond Running

Cross-Training and Fitness

Every time you run, you strengthen your heart, lungs, muscles, even your brain. On any given run you also tighten muscles, stress joints, and do all sorts of other minor damage that adds up over time. It just comes with the territory—all those steps accumulate in both good ways and bad. As you build up your body, you beat it up a little along the way.

If you train on trails, you're already one step ahead of most runners when it comes to taking care of yourself. Soft trails are far more forgiving than hard road surfaces. And since trails offer more terrain variety, your feet and legs don't suffer the same stress associated with the repetitive motion of road running.

Still, running is notorious for tightening muscles and developing some parts of the body at the expense of others. If you want to remain a healthy runner, supplement with other exercise and take care of yourself with some commonsense maintenance to counterbalance the worst of the sport's offenses. If you take the time to mix it up, you'll see the payoff in your running performance, your overall health, and your ability to maintain a running program with fewer injuries and downtime. Stretching, strength training, and other activities can alleviate running-related troubles such as muscle imbalances, tightness, and injuries from overuse.

Stretching

Stretching keeps muscles loose and limber. Flexible muscles allow for optimal range of motion and reaction while you're running, which translates to better performance. Loose muscles are also less prone to such injuries as pulls and tears and can keep even more serious injuries of the connective tissue at bay. Common running overuse injuries such as Achilles tendonitis, patella (kneecap) pain, and plantar fasciitis often can be traced back to tight muscles that resulted in an abbreviated and corrupted stride or placed excessive stress on ligaments and tendons.

The running world is full of athletes who learn too late—after serious injury—the importance of stretching.

A daily stretching routine needn't take a lot of time, but it should include all the major muscle groups. Runners are prone to having tight muscles in general, and tight hamstrings and gluteus muscles in particular. Less obvious areas of the body tighten from running as well, however, so it's important to stretch all areas, including the back, abdomen, shoulders, and calves. By stretching well after workouts you can avoid much of the stiffness that would otherwise set in by the following day. And you do need to stretch every time you run—once a week or so isn't enough to see flexibility benefits if you run every day.

Stretching styles have come and gone over the years. In the old days, you might have been admonished to stretch *before* exercise— stretching itself was considered a warmup. However, we now know that stretching without any previous activity can lead to strains and tears. Instead, get some blood flowing into your muscles prior to stretching. That means instead of stretching before your run, do it afterward. Prepare for

Stretching Your Limit

It turns out that even such a benign practice as stretching can sometimes offer too much of a good thing. It's tempting to stretch your muscles to the point of pain or to try to increase flexibility when a muscle is sore. But that can cause or aggravate an injury. Remember: Stretch gently. And if you're nursing an injury, you'll do it more good by stretching the nearby muscles, ensuring healthy range of motion without tugging on a spot that's already tender.

a race or tough workout by walking or jogging a few slow miles to warm up and then stretch thoroughly before you do your fast running.

Bouncing during stretching (otherwise known as ballistic stretching), once a popular method thought to optimize a stretch, should be avoided because it increases the likelihood of injury. Instead, stretch to the point of comfortable tension and hold the position for anywhere from 20 seconds to 1 minute. If this hurts, the stretch position is too extreme—stretch only as far as you can comfortably. After 30 seconds or so, you can back off the stretch and stretch the opposite side. Return to the same stretch on the other side if you wish, and increase your range of motion each time, but always hold the stretch gently without strain or bouncing.

The following stretches provide a good basic routine to get you started.

STRETCHES

HAMSTRING

Lie down on your back with both legs extended. (1) Bend your left leg at the knee and gently pull it toward your chest. Hold for a few seconds. (2) Then extend your left leg straight so it is perpendicular to the ground. Gently pull the leg toward your body, as far as you can comfortably hold it while keeping it straight. Do not raise your lower back off the ground. Hold, then switch legs.

QUADRICEPS

Lie on the floor on your right side. (1) Bend your right leg at the knee, and stabilize yourself by grabbing and holding that knee with your right hand. (2) Bend the left leg at the knee and grab your foot with your left

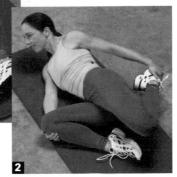

hand. Gently pull your left foot and leg toward the buttocks, and feel the stretch along the front of your leg. Hold, then switch sides.

CALF

Stand about a foot away from a wall or a pole and place both hands on the wall at about shoulder level. (1) Step back with your right leg and bend your left knee. Keeping your right leg straight, gently stretch the calf area. (2) Then

bend your right knee and gently stretch your lower calf area. (Be sure not to let the foot of your back leg roll inward, which will tug on your plantar fascia.) Hold, then switch legs.

HIP AND SIDE

Stand at arm's length from a stationary object, resting your right hand on it for support. Cross your left leg in front of your right leg. Raise your left arm and curve your body toward the wall to create an arc from the tips of your fingers down to your feet. Press your left hip out as far as is comfortable. Hold, then repeat on the right side.

BUTTOCKS

Lie on the ground with your knees bent and feet on the floor. (1) Cross your left leg over your right, so the left ankle rests above your right knee. (2) Lift both legs off the floor, grasping your right knee with your right hand, and your right foot with your left hand. Gently pull your legs toward your chest. Hold, then switch legs.

GROIN AREA

Sit on the floor with your knees bent and the soles of your feet pressed together. With your hands on your ankles, let your knees drop gently toward the floor. Keep your back straight. Hold; do not push, force, or bounce.

ARM/SHOULDER

Grab a pole or sturdy object with your right hand. (1) Keeping your right arm straight, slightly turn your body to the left and feel the stretch in your biceps and shoulder. (2) Then release the pole and cross your right arm in front of your body, cradling it from underneath with your left arm, and gently tug it across your body. Hold, and repeat with your left arm.

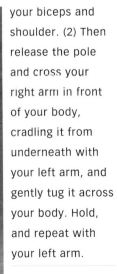

1

2

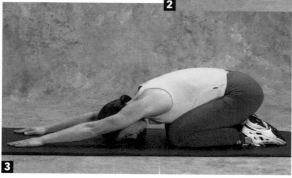

3

ABDOMEN AND BACK

Lie facedown on the ground with your legs extended behind you. Place your palms on the floor just outside your shoulders. (1) Slowly arch your back and lift your upper body by extending your arms straight. Hold the position, but do not force it if your back hurts.

Follow the abdominal stretch with its counterpart for the back. (2) From this position, rise up on your hands and knees. (3) Slowly shift your buttocks back and down until your legs are folded under you. Your buttocks will rest on your heels, your chest on your upper thighs, and your arms will extend straight out in front. Hold.

Strength Training

Mile upon mile of running will help you build tremendous endurance, but not necessarily explosive strength or well-proportioned muscles. Strength training can round out your physical fitness by helping you develop power and evenly balanced muscle groups.

Trail runners can benefit from full-body strength. Powerful legs help conquer hilly courses. Core strength—strong abdominal and back muscles—is critical for maintaining efficient upright posture over long periods of time. Even arms can get fatigued on long runs, so it doesn't hurt to make them strong. And a strong upper body—both your core and your arms—is helpful in maintaining balance on tricky downhill stretches of trail.

Evenly developed muscles can help you run better, but even more important, they can actually keep you free from injury. That's because if one muscle consistently overpowers another, it can pull your running stride out of alignment, tugging on weaker muscles or connective tissue. For example, some road runners suffer deterioration of the patella (kneecap) from improper tracking of the knee when overdeveloped hamstrings don't allow the weaker quadriceps to hold the knee in proper alignment.

The opposite case—with a different outcome—can occur in trail runners with overdeveloped quads, says Stephanie Ehret, a competitive trail runner and certified massage therapist who works primarily on runners. "If you develop really strong quads, it pulls the pelvis forward and puts torque on the hamstrings. Your hamstrings feel tight, but they're actually weakened. The worst thing you can do is constantly stretch them, since that keeps pulling the pelvis forward." Instead, she says, the answer is to strengthen your hamstrings to restore balance. (Trail runners do more hill climbing than other runners, so they tend to overdevelop their quadriceps. Conversely, road runners overdevelop their hamstrings at the expense of their quads.)

The more running you do, the greater your risk for imbalance injuries. That's because more miles translate to greater stress on the body. Almost all serious runners, especially those experiencing the onset of pain, can benefit from a muscle-balance analysis performed by an experienced trainer or sports physical therapist (at a health club or sports medicine center) who can then recommend specific strengthening exercises for you to counteract any imbalances.

When it comes to strength training, you can choose from numerous methods. The most typical is traditional weight training, either with machines or free weights. The machines you find at health clubs are excellent at isolating particular muscles. They provide a good starting point for beginners who otherwise might not know which exercises to do or how to perform them correctly. With machines, you can follow the circuit already provided at your health club and you'll work most of your muscle groups.

Free weights—dumbbells that go in each hand or barbells that can be set to varying weights depending on the number of plates added on—are more challenging. They don't have a pulley system to help control the exercise, which means your smaller, surrounding muscles need to work harder as your body stabilizes the weight. It's harder to "cheat" with free weights, meaning that both sides of your body must work equally to successfully execute an exercise. (Your body's stronger side can sometimes compensate for its weaker side when you use a weight machine.) The drawbacks of using free weights include a greater chance that you won't maintain proper form and that you'll need a spotter for some exercises to ensure you don't drop the weight. If you're new to strength training, ask for assistance at your health club or gym.

Beyond tossing around iron in a gym, you can strengthen your body in other ways. Resistance bands (as the name implies) provide resistance that your body's muscles must work against. Working with pulleys, stretch cords, and resistance balls, all of which are sold at sporting goods stores, have similar benefits. You also can use your body's own weight as resistance in such traditional exercises as pullups, pushups, and abdominal crunches.

The goal of strength training for runners is not to build tremendous bulk or lifting capability. You should use light to moderate weights to avoid adding unnecessary size, which doesn't benefit running performance. Shoot for anywhere from 10 to 15 repetitions of a particular exercise. You can do one, two, or three sets of all your exercises, but one set is enough for fitness gains. Plan on lifting two or three times a week; less than that isn't enough for you to see significant benefits, and more than that won't allow for proper rest and recovery.

If you're a competitive runner, concentrate most of your strength training in the off-season. After that you'll maintain the strength you need for your racing season. Once you're training seriously for competition, you won't want to expend energy on strength training—and your legs may be too tired for such a workout, anyway.

The following workout is designed specifically for trail runners and concentrates on developing core and lower body strength. It places special emphasis on strengthening ankles and feet, along with developing the exceptional balance you need for staying upright on the trail. The only piece of equipment you'll need is some resistance tubing, which you can find at a sporting goods store. That means you can do this workout at home and at your convenience, rather than relying on a health club membership. Follow the above guidelines for sets and repetitions.

CORE AND UPPER BODY

PUSHUP

This old standby is still one of
the best upper body and core
strengtheners. Lie facedown
resting your palms on the floor
beside your shoulders. (1) Keeping your back and legs straight, extend your arms to
lift your body off the floor. (2) Slowly lower yourself to within a few inches of the
floor and repeat. If you have difficulty completing just one or two pushups, work up
to these by bending your legs and resting your knees on the floor while you raise
and lower your body.

ABDOMINAL CRUNCH

(1) Lie on your back, knees bent and feet
flat on the floor. Cross your arms in front
of you and rest them lightly on your chest.
(2) Slowly raise your upper body toward your
knees until only your lower back remains on
the ground. (Your arms, head, and
chest should not meet your knees,
and your shoulders should come up
only about a foot to a foot and a half
off the ground.) Lower your upper
body slowly to the floor and repeat.
Resist the urge to do these quickly:
Jerking yourself up and down doesn't
work your muscles efficiently.

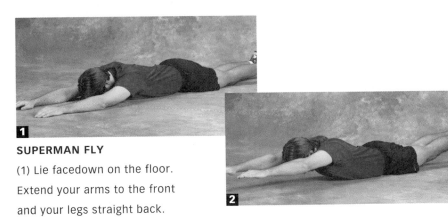

SUPERMAN FLY

(1) Lie facedown on the floor.
Extend your arms to the front
and your legs straight back.

(2) Contract your abdominal muscles and then lift both legs and both arms off the
floor a few inches. Hold for 30 seconds or as long as you can. Repeat.

TRICEPS DIP

Sit on the edge of a sturdy,
stationary bench or chair with your
hands at your sides grasping the
edge. (1) Slowly "walk" your feet out
in front of you and lift your buttocks
off the bench so that you are
supporting yourself with your hands.
Your arms should be straight and
your body in a straight line. (2) Raise
and lower your
body— holding it
straight—by bending
your arms and then
straightening them.

LOWER BODY

STABILIZER

This deceptively simple move targets your midsection, buttocks, and upper legs. Lie facedown on the ground, with your feet together and your palms down just outside your shoulders. (1) Keeping your body straight, raise yourself up into a pushup position. (2) With your body in a straight line, lift one leg off the ground and hold 5 seconds, contracting your abdominal, buttocks, and leg muscles. Repeat on the other side.

LEG EXTENSION

This is a version of the quadriceps-building leg extension typically done on a machine. (1) Sit on a chair or bench with your feet on the floor a few inches apart. Wrap resistance tubing around both ankles and around the chair legs below you. Grip the seat with your hands for balance. (2) Slowly straighten your legs out in front of you until you feel maximum resistance from the band. Lower your legs, and repeat. (You can also perform this exercise one leg at a time.)

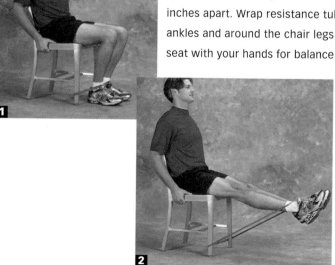

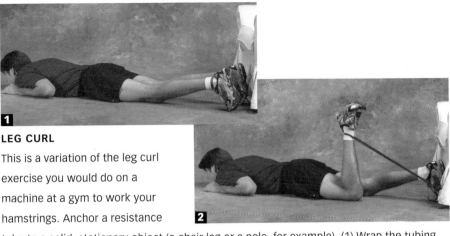

LEG CURL

This is a variation of the leg curl exercise you would do on a machine at a gym to work your hamstrings. Anchor a resistance tube to a solid, stationary object (a chair leg or a pole, for example). (1) Wrap the tubing around one ankle and lie facedown on the ground with your legs extended behind you; your body should point away from the chair or pole. Adjust your body position so that the tubing is fairly taut. (2) Bend your leg at the knee and raise your foot toward your buttocks until it is perpendicular to the ground. Slowly lower and repeat with the other leg.

LATERAL LEG STRENGTHENER

Anchor a resistance tube to a sturdy, stationary item like a chair. Stand sideways to the point of resistance and loop the band around your outside leg. (1) Grab the chair to prevent yourself from leaning and push your leg out a few inches in front of your body. Then, swing it away from the point of resistance about 8 to 10 inches to work your outer thigh. (2) To work your inner thigh, loop the band around your inner ankle and swing your leg (again, slightly in front of your body) across your body as far as you can away from the anchor point.

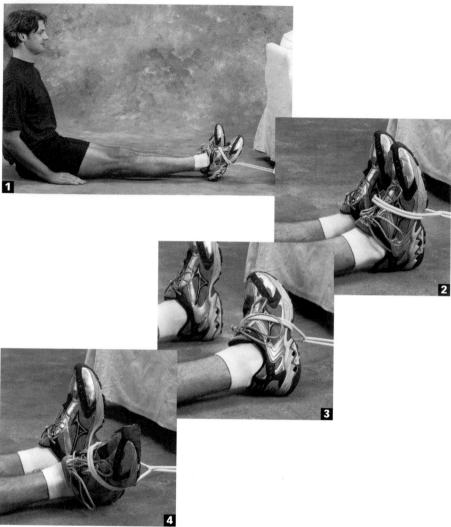

ANKLE STRENGTHENER I

Attach a resistance band to a chair leg or other sturdy anchor. (1) Sit on the floor facing the point of resistance with your legs extended in front of you. Loop the band around the middle of one foot. (2) From a pointed position, flex your foot to pull against the point of resistance. (3) Then, bend your foot sideways at the ankle, first pointing your foot left, (4) then right. Repeat with the other foot.

ANKLE STRENGTHENERS II

(1) Hold a resistance band in your hands and sit on the floor with your legs extended in front of you.
(2) Loop the band around the middle of one foot and point your foot down. Repeat with the other foot.

BONUS EXERCISE: BALANCE BUILDER

This is the one time I'll recommend buying a piece of equipment for a specific exercise. Wobble boards consist of a small platform with half a sphere attached to the bottom. They are terrific for developing overall balance as well as the small muscles in your feet, ankles, and lower legs that you recruit in the act of balancing. Strengthening these muscles and your coordination means you'll react better to obstacles on the trail and run more securely. Buy a balance board at your local sporting goods store then take it home and play. Your goal: Stay standing.

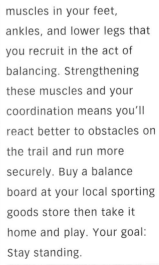

Cross-Training Options

As people have come to understand the benefits of not doing the same exercise every day, cross-training has grown in popularity. Mixing the right sports together allows your body to rest the muscles that work overtime during running. At the same time, supplementary activities can also work the other muscles that running doesn't emphasize. Beyond the physical benefits, cross-training creates a mental break from the running routine, which means you're more likely to feel fresh for your next running workout.

Activities that create less impact on the legs and are less weight-bearing than running complement it most effectively. As it turns out, these activities include just about everything from cycling to cross-country skiing to in-line skating. Even hiking is a good choice at times, since it creates less impact than running. Or you can switch the focus

tip of the trail

Competing Options

The amount of running required for competitive racing demands a tremendous amount of energy—and energy used for other sports detracts from running workouts. So the more competitive a runner you are, the less time you'll want to spend cross-training. That said, even serious runners can benefit from activities such as swimming or Pilates on their easy days. The key is to choose activities that stretch and strengthen muscles at the same time. The last thing a serious runner needs is to undertake activities that lead to greater muscle tightness.

away from your legs and give the rest of your body a workout with activities such as swimming, yoga, or Pilates.

Cross-training is a terrific way to maintain fitness during periods when running isn't an option. During injury rehabilitation, for example, you can choose an activity that doesn't stress the injured body part. Swimming, cycling, and water jogging can be good options, depending on your injury. They will help you maintain cardiovascular and muscular fitness during weeks or months of running downtime.

Finally, the older you are, the more cross-training makes sense for you. Stories abound of running purists who scoffed at the idea of cross-training in youth, only to become converts later in life. That's because as an aging body becomes less forgiving and more prone to injury, cross-training can ease the wear and tear of running.

Pilates and Yoga

Both exercise disciplines make a terrific counterpart to running. The benefit lies in their ability to build muscle strength while simultaneously increasing range of motion and flexibility. Runners often feel uncomfortable when first undertaking Pilates or yoga classes because they tend to be tight and inflexible and have trouble with some positions. Stay in class long enough to reap the benefits, though, and you'll likely become addicted to the feeling of flexibility, strength, relaxation, and even improved posture that these popular activities impart.

Cycling

Cycling is a good option for injured runners who want to maintain leg strength and for runners with underdeveloped quadriceps. Conversely, trail runners who do a lot of mountainous climbing and already have strong quads may want to go easy on this sport. Cycling is muscularly intensive, working most of the lower body, the lower back, and, when climbing hills, the upper body as well. If you want a cycling workout to replace your running workout, plan on spending more time on the bike than you would on your feet. The equivalent cycling workout should be about three to four times the length of your run.

Swimming

Swimming is a classic cross-training activity for runners. Easy on the joints and feet, working the arms and torso, swimming is a great choice when you feel the need to give your body a rest and do something completely different from running. Swimming also stretches the body instead of tightening it, a nice benefit for chronically stiff runners. Because swimming is gentle and complementary to running, you can double up on your workout days if you like and go for a swim after you run.

Water Running

Running in the water is dull but effective. Water running allows an athlete to very closely approximate the motion of running with no impact on the legs. That makes it good fitness maintenance for runners who have stress fractures or other lower body injuries. The water's resistance makes for an even more muscularly intense total-body workout than running on land. But because of its monotonous nature, usually only more serious runners do it, and then only during injury rehabilitation.

Since it's not commonly done, here's some instruction on effective water running. Most runners who try this type of cross-training will want to wear a flotation device specially designed for water running. While it's more challenging to run in the water without one of these belts, it's also virtually impossible to stay afloat long enough for a workout.

The pool must be deep enough for you to "run" in without letting your feet touch the bottom. You can do many of the same types of workouts in the water as you would on the trail, including tempo runs and intervals. (Because you can't gauge your workout by distance covered, use your watch as you would on the trail.) Warm up with slow jogging, and then pump faster to duplicate your land workouts. You can increase the intensity of your workout by speeding up the frequency of leg turnover, but you won't necessarily cover ground any faster. In fact, if you're running with proper form—that is, the same upright posture you'd have on land—you won't cover much ground at all. (Some runners lean too far forward in the water because it allows them to cover more ground, and end up in a doggy paddle. They negate the benefits of the activity, which come from closely approximating the running stride, and not from flailing around in any old fashion.)

Cross-Country Skiing

Nordic skiing is very similar to running in the way it develops your legs and cardiovascular system. And it comes with the bonus of having virtually no impact on the joints. That makes it a nice off-season break for those of you who live in colder climates, allowing you to burn calories and stay fit without having to run in uncomfortable or dangerous conditions. Be cautious when returning to running after a winter of skiing, though: Your joints will need to readjust gradually to the pounding of running, even if you stick to the trails.

Snowshoeing

If you want a good winter substitute for trail running, you can't get much closer to the real thing than snowshoeing. With a pair of snow-

When Trail Running
Is Your Cross-Training

Running is one of the best fitness builders that exists. You can't beat it for burning calories, building endurance, and developing your cardiovascular system. That's why athletes in just about every sport incorporate running into their training. And since trail running provides greater variety of muscle development and is easier on the legs, leading to fewer injuries, it's a good cross-training option.

Triathletes and adventure racers in particular have discovered the benefits of trail running. Off-road triathlons, which require mountain-bike and trail-running segments instead of doing both on the road, have become a popular division of the sport. Training for these races requires an athlete to train on trails to get ready for different types of terrain during competition. And adventure racers, who sometimes don't know how they'll be asked to cover terrain, make trail running a training staple that serves as a strengthening and endurance base for everything else.

If you want to include trail running as part of an overall fitness program that involves many different activities, strive to run at least three times a week. Running less than that will make it more difficult for your body to adjust to the sport, and you'll also be less likely to reap the physiological benefits of running. Alternate sports or activities so that you stress different body parts or systems on alternate days. And when you do run, add variety. Just because running isn't your primary sport doesn't mean you have to run 45 boring, flat-paced minutes every time you head out. Throw some tempo runs, fartlek, or hills into the mix, and you'll build your speed and keep it fun at the same time.

shoes designed specifically for speed, you can run in the snow using a very natural stride. Snowshoeing is a terrific cardiovascular conditioner, and it's also a very intense muscular workout. If you want your snowshoeing session to approximate your regular running workouts, plan on heading out for as long as you would run, or a bit longer (since you'll be going slower). You can even do interval or hill workouts on your snowshoes. Because regular trail markers are often covered in the snow, it's easy to feel as if you can go anywhere on snowshoes. Be creative and have fun—just be cautious and respectful of private and public land boundaries if you decide to break your own trail.

CHAPTER ELEVEN

Fuel for the Trail

The Runner's Diet

L et's start with the payoff you've been waiting for: Runners can get away with murder when it comes to their diets. Think of all the calories you burn! Your endlessly stoked metabolism! Your smug satisfaction when grabbing a doughnut and telling yourself, "I *need* the fat."

Okay, stop patting yourself on the back now. Here's the rest of the story. Yes, you buy yourself a little leeway by exercising regularly. You do burn more calories than your sedentary office mates, and you're probably leaner and stronger than most folks you know. But if you use that as license to binge, you're not doing your body any favors. Even if you don't have to worry about your weight, the general rules of nutrition still apply to you. You may feel invincible because you're a runner, but you still should eat right.

Eating right isn't just about how many calories you take in and how many you burn off. The quality of the fuel you consume has everything to do with muscle strength, organ function, bone density, and immune-system health—not to mention running performance and recovery. A steady diet of fast food and candy bars not only keeps you from reaching your running potential, it also saps you of energy and puts you at risk for heart disease and diabetes. A healthy diet full of nutrients and vitamins, conversely, ensures optimal performance for your running and helps you combat colds, fatigue, stress, and serious illness.

The best diet for a runner is much the same as the best diet for everybody. Diet books and magazines will try to sell you some other truth—there's no shortage of books with titles like *The Athlete's Miracle Protein Performance Cure*, or some permutation of those words. But eating nothing but steak, or pineapple, or whatever is the latest craze won't make you faster. Eating right as a runner means eating right in general.

Eating Well

It doesn't take an advanced degree to plan a healthy menu. The general principles of nutrition are the basic concepts you've always heard, starting with your mother's admonition to eat your vegetables.

So why are our diets so unhealthy?

We're up against a slew of forces that are counterproductive to the basics of healthy eating. We don't have time to cook at home. It's more convenient to pick up something that's already prepared. Fast food is cheap. Quality produce can be expensive. Portions everywhere have ballooned. Few people eat at the table anymore, choosing to eat in front of the TV or computer instead. The list goes on and on—and so does the list of health problems reaching epidemic proportions as a result of high-fat diets and expanding waistlines.

There's no secret solution to the problem. Flashy new weight-loss or energy-boosting pills, tricks, and shortcuts often aren't backed up by research. The real answer is the one that doesn't sell books or magazines: Eat smart. Eat less (or run more). Cook at home more. Stop thinking about it so much. You can get bogged down trying to measure all sorts of percentages and calories at the kitchen counter, but it's really not necessary. Just get back to the basics—eat plenty of fresh produce and complex carbohydrates; lean, healthy protein sources; and fats and sweets in moderation.

Of course, it's easy to lose track of the basics in the muddle of news about fad diets. So here are some very simple, commonsense ways to understand the most important principles about eating right:

Get a lot of carbohydrates, enough protein, and a little fat. Forget 40-30-30, 70-20-10, or other ratios you've read about in diet or training books. Honestly, when was the last time you weighed your food and calculated these numbers meal after meal? It's more helpful to think of the way you divide the food on your plate. The bulk of your meal should consist of carbohydrates from sources like grains, vegetables, and fruits. A smaller portion of the meal should come from healthy protein sources: fish, chicken, lean meats, beans, tofu, and low-fat dairy sources. And the smallest portion should consist of fats and sweets, which should be consumed mainly as condiments or seasonings.

Americans tend to either overdose on protein—as in the 2-inch-thick Porterhouse—or ignore it altogether—eating the Caesar salad for dinner. Strive for moderate portions of healthy proteins and avoid feast or famine.

Eat more healthy fats and fewer of the less-healthy variety. All fat is not created equal. Saturated fats are the bad guys, clogging arteries, raising cholesterol levels, and putting you at risk for heart disease. Examples are butter, fat found in beef, and coconut oil. Replace such fats with healthier choices whenever possible. Olive and canola oils top the list of choices, followed by corn, safflower, and sunflower oils. It's not necessary, or even desirable, to eliminate fat altogether. We need fat to fuel our bodies, especially when exercising vigorously. Just try to get fat from good sources such as nuts and fish instead of from a side order of fries.

Eat low on the food chain. The more that has been done to your food before it reaches your plate, the less chance it has of being healthy. Processed foods retain only minimal nutrients and fiber and are pumped full of fat and sodium. As an alternative to processed sugared cereal, cook whole oats for breakfast. Instead of buying store-bought cookies, which brim with hydrogenated fats and excess sugar, choose fruit or home-baked, whole-grain muffins for dessert. This principle works across the food spectrum, whether it's simply eating brown rice instead of processed white rice, wheat bread instead of white, or whole fruit instead of juice, which lacks the fiber of the original fruit.

Get a lot of variety. The more types of foods you eat, the greater the variety of nutrients you'll take in. Also, you'll be more likely to satisfy your desire for flavor, making you less likely to binge on unhealthy treats. Lots of people get into a rut, eating the same things day after day. Force yourself to try new things by buying an unfamiliar item once a week at the grocery store, or by ordering something different from the menu at your favorite lunch spot. The flip side to this rule of thumb is not to exclude too many foods from your diet. If you cut back on red meat, remember that it's fine and even healthy to have some lean beef in your diet. Likewise, you might not want an omelet every morning, but there's no need to eliminate eggs altogether.

Don't diet; just eat well. A diet implies a controlled, temporary fix to a problem. That means it also implies an end point, after which all bets are off and you return to grabbing whatever garbage food is handy. Eating well, on the other hand, means a lifetime of healthy choices. Think of eating well not as a form of deprivation, but as a decision to choose fresh, delicious food that also happens to provide optimal nutrition. It should offer enough variety and satisfaction to make you feel full and happy in the long term. As with running, the great thing about eating right is that your body adjusts to what you throw at it—once you get used to eating well, stuffing yourself with sodden sweets and fats won't appeal to you anymore.

Vitamin Supplements

Athletes love pills. We've been told that mega-doses of vitamin C stave off colds, B vitamins produce energy, zinc aids recovery, and on, and on. Take a closer look at the facts: There's no proof that popping endless vitamin C will keep you from getting sick. Vitamins alone don't give you any energy, since they contain no calories. And too much zinc, like other nonsoluble minerals, can be dangerous.

The subject of vitamins is rife with misinformation. Athletes fall prey because they want a quick fix, a magic pill that will catapult their performance to a new level. They may think they need extra vitamins because their bodies work extra hard. Or that if a little bit of a vitamin or mineral is good, a lot is better.

Put simply: Vitamins don't work that way.

Yes, the body needs vitamins and minerals to function properly. But a healthy diet should provide the body with what it needs in terms of these requirements. Boosting levels beyond this does not guarantee superior performance. In fact, some vitamins and minerals can be toxic at high doses, or at the very least, they can interfere with the absorption of other vitamins and minerals.

The smartest approach to vitamin supplements is to do just what the name implies: supplement. Think of pills as an addition to your diet, not as its foundation. Reliable sports nutritionists typically recommend a simple vitamin and mineral supplement with antioxidants (and, for women, with calcium) to runners as an insurance policy in case you fall short in some area of nutritional requirement. You don't need megadoses of anything or 10 different pills the size of your pinkie.

Yes, it's true that running and other intensive exercise can increase

Four Rules for Eating Right

These simple strategies take the chore out of eating well:

1. EAT YOUR BREAKFAST. Eating first thing in the morning revs your metabolism, giving you energy for both work and working out. It also lessens the chance that you'll be famished later in the day and overeat at dinner, when your willpower wanes. Dieters are notorious breakfast skippers; not coincidentally, they're also notorious late-night bingers. Making healthy choices for breakfast is very simple. Toss together some whole-grain cereal, low-fat milk, and fruit and you've got a healthy meal. If you're running late, blend a smoothie with yogurt, banana, and juice. Then grab a bagel on your way out the door.

2. SNEAK YOUR FRUITS AND VEGGIES. You don't have to munch on raw carrots if you're not a vegetable fan. Add finely diced vegetables to your spaghetti sauce or soup—you'll barely notice them. Chop some greens and add them to your rice when it's almost finished cooking. Blend fresh fruit into your smoothies. Include dried fruit in baked goods and salads.

the body's need for certain vitamins and minerals. But in general, this kind of intensive exercise also increases the appetite. So when an athlete expends extra calories, he or she will likely eat more food. That means any additional nutritional requirements are probably being met by eating more.

If you're still convinced that you require more than a general multivitamin with antioxidants, see a nutritionist to map out a customized action plan. You're better off getting informed advice for a safe vitamin strategy than you are grabbing a few bottles here and a few more there, adding to your arsenal every time you read an article about the

3. CHOOSE GOOD SNACKS. If your stomach is rumbling at 3:00 P.M., don't ignore it. Snacking can keep you from overeating later in the day. Keep healthy snacks on hand so you don't end up staring down a candy-filled vending machine. Try a bagel with peanut butter, yogurt with nuts, or a bowl of cereal with milk. Endurance-sports nutritionist Alice Lindeman, Ph.D., R.D., recommends following this simple snacking rule: Include at least two food groups each time you snack. For example, instead of having just an apple, eat an apple with some cottage cheese. "This forces you to eat different types of foods and forces you to eat the food pyramid without thinking about it," Lindeman explains.

4. TRY THE 90/10 RULE. Be good 90 percent of the time in your eating choices. Then allow yourself to splurge 10 percent of the time. This method keeps you from feeling deprived and provides a built-in relief valve that means you're more likely to stick to your healthy choices. If you never allow yourself a burger and fries or a piece of cheesecake, you're going to feel cheated and obsess over such indulgences—and eventually you'll fall off the wagon.

wondrous effect of mineral XYZ. The risk in this hit-or-miss method is that you could take potentially hazardous amounts by combining pills and accidentally doubling up on doses. Also, a large dose of one vitamin or mineral can interfere with the effectiveness of another.

Water and Hydration

Your body is much more forgiving when it comes to food than it is with that other piece of the fuel puzzle: water. The only thing our bodies demand more regularly than water is air. If only we were as consistent about drinking as we are about breathing. In fact, many people walk

tip of the trail

Getting a Grip on Iron

Iron is one of the trickier minerals to get a handle on. Women are prone to iron deficiency and therefore should take a supplement that includes iron. Conversely, men have a lower iron requirement and are more susceptible to iron overload (which is dangerous to heart health), so their supplements shouldn't include the mineral.

Running throws another variable into the mix: Distance running can deplete iron reserves, both through sweat and muscle stress that damages red blood cells. Therefore, some male runners may need more iron in their diets or a supplement with iron. If you're male and are doing serious marathon training, consider getting your blood checked to see which side of the iron equation you fall on. Women certainly can be tested too, but most women can't go wrong taking a multivitamin that contains iron.

around in a chronic state of semidehydration. They don't realize that a simple chug of water could alleviate their low-grade headache, fatigue, or irritability. And that's just the sedentary folk.

Athletes who flirt with dehydration face a far more serious set of dangers: Extreme dehydration during a sporting event or workout can result in increased body temperature, cramps, nausea, and eventually, heat exhaustion or life-threatening heatstroke. It goes without saying that athletic performance is impaired at this point as well, but that's the least of your worries when you're lying in the medical tent attached to an intravenous drip.

The best defense against dehydration is to drink regularly throughout the day. Athletes are often admonished to drink a bottle of water before and after exercise, but as I've said earlier in this book, it's overall water intake that's important. Besides, too much water prior to a run will slosh around in your stomach uncomfortably. Your strategy as a runner should be to hydrate constantly throughout the day. Drink when you get up in the morning, when you take a break at work, when you eat, and before bed. And sure, drink before and after your runs, too.

The often-cited goal of drinking eight glasses of water a day, by the way, is actually too low a target for endurance athletes; it's a figure more accurate for sedentary people. And besides, as with food, you're not likely to measure how much you drink every day.

So how do you know how much to drink? Some runners like to weigh themselves before and after a long run. That way you can see how much weight you've lost in sweat and then drink yourself back up to your prerun weight. A simpler method is to check your urine: The color should be light and clear. Dark yellow urine is a sign of dehydration. And don't think you can trust your thirst to tell you when to drink. Thirst is a latent indicator of dehydration—by the time you're thirsty, you're already dehydrated.

Water isn't your only option for hydrating. Most liquids that don't contain caffeine are fine choices: juice, soup, and smoothies all provide lots of water. You'll find countless sports drinks for athletes, too. These beverages typically contain some form of sugar and sodium as a carbohydrate and electrolyte source to fuel your muscles during exercise and replenish them afterward. Whether these are right for you depends on how much you run and how much money you like to spend.

If you run for less than an hour, you really don't need sports drinks. Your body hasn't significantly depleted its carbohydrate stores, and water is fine for simple rehydration. When your runs go beyond an hour, you begin to burn your glycogen stores and a sports drink makes sense.

Each runner develops his own preference when it comes to sports drinks—you'll probably want to test several different brands and flavors. Many athletes prefer these drinks at a weaker concentration than recommended by the manufacturer, so experiment with watering them down, too. You can also create your own sports drink by diluting juice or drinking flat soda. Manufacturers want you to believe that rigorous science has created the perfect performance booster, which can be yours for a couple of bucks a bottle, but individual bodies react so differently that what works wonders for one runner won't be palatable for another. Sometimes there's more marketing than magic in those bottles.

Eating before Your Run

Prerun eating habits are highly individual. Some runners seem to have cast-iron stomachs—they think nothing of heading out for an hour's run right after downing a plate of spaghetti and tomato sauce. Other runners carefully monitor everything they eat—or don't eat at all—for hours before running. Whichever camp you fall into is partially the luck of the draw, but it's also related to your fitness level: The more training you do, the more your digestive tract will learn to handle.

Ideally, your stomach should be neither empty nor full when you set out on a run. Running on a full stomach is an invitation to digestive troubles, and running on an empty stomach can leave you too weak for your workout. If you've had a full, heavy meal, leave at least 3 to 4 hours to digest it before exercising. On the other hand, if you haven't eaten at all for several hours before your run (or if you're running first thing in the morning), eat a light snack 30 minutes to an hour before you run. Otherwise low blood sugar can impair your ability to run optimally.

Good prerun food choices include plain-tasting, high-carb, low-fiber snacks. A bagel, sports bar, and toast are safe choices; many runners like something bread-y before running because they think such

tip of the trail

Too Much of a Good Thing

A final word about hydration: Hyponatremia. "Hypo-huh?" you ask. It's a fancy way of saying low blood sodium, and it occurs when excessive sweat loss is replaced by taking in only plain water. While most runners will never run long or hard enough to put themselves at risk of hyponatremia, it's a sneaky condition that can occur, ironically, when you're trying hard to stay hydrated. Several hours into a long run you might feel a little weak and dizzy and assume you're dehydrated, so you drink more water. And more. And more. But the problem is that if you're not also taking in some salt, you're essentially overdosing on water. Low blood sodium most commonly occurs, not surprisingly, among athletes in endurance events such as ultramarathons and long-distance triathlons. Symptoms include nausea, headache, muscle cramps, and confusion.

To be safe, during any run or multisport competition lasting more than 90 minutes, drink sports drinks, diluted juice, or soup, or eat something salty, such as pretzels, with your water.

items absorb excess stomach acids. Bananas are the best fruit choice for most runners. Anything too high in fiber can lead to bowel difficulties on the run. Likewise, lots of liquid (think grapes or melon) can slosh around and lead to stomach cramps and uncomfortable bloating. Stay away from excess fat or protein before running, because they're harder to digest. And avoid anything spicy or gassy before you run.

If you usually don't eat before running, you can slowly train your body to tolerate food and drink. Start by eating a few bites of bread and a sip of water a half-hour before your run. Slowly increase the amount you eat and drink before each run by taking in a little bit more each day. Eventually, you'll be able to stomach a greater variety of items. And chances are your running will improve when you're no longer running on empty.

Eating after Your Run

Most runners aren't hungry right after a run, but it's actually important to take in some nutrients as soon as possible after your workout. That's because there's a window of time immediately after exertion during which the body is best able to absorb nutrients and replenish glycogen stores. This window of time is about 60 to 90 minutes long, but the sooner you take in the food within that time frame, the better.

Eating a postrun snack immediately after running helps restore hydration, rebuild muscle protein, boost glycogen stores, and fend off immune system suppression. That translates into less muscle soreness and fatigue, and better performance on your next run. The harder, longer, and more often you run, the more important this becomes. If you're running every day—or even twice on some days—your muscles don't have much time to recover. (If you're running only every other day, your muscles have plenty of time to recover and refuel.)

For optimal refueling and recovery, your meal or snack should include fluids, carbohydrates, electrolytes, and protein. That sounds like a lot, but with a little planning, you can easily cover all those bases. Try a smoothie made with yogurt, orange juice, and banana. Or a bagel with peanut butter and jelly, partnered with water or juice. On a cold day, chicken noodle soup fits the bill.

Remember, the 60- to 90-minute time frame is critical for optimal recovery, especially when you train hard. So even if you plan to eat a full meal eventually after you shower and get dressed, grab a quick balanced snack first.

Specialized Sports Fuels

Foods created specifically for sports have become big business. You'll find dozens of sports bars and gels on the shelves of your local running store, promising quick energy and even quicker recovery to those who indulge. Do they work? Sure, some do. Are they convenient? Of course—that's their main appeal. Do you really need to spend a buck and a half for some carbs? Not really.

The real selling point of sports bars is that they're neatly packaged calorie bundles. They're great for when you don't have time to consider a proper pre-workout snack or you want a familiar, easily portable, safe-for-your-stomach prerace meal. If it's a bar or nothing at all, grab the bar. But their makers' claims about performance boosting are dubious. If a bar contains vitamins, that's great, but a regular supplement is a cheaper way to get the same benefits. (Besides, no amount of vitamins will help

Trail Etiquette

Clean Fueling

A nasty side effect of sports-gel proliferation is roadsides and trails littered with little foil packets. Gel holsters— little plastic vials that strap onto your waist belt or fit into your pack —solve the problem. Simply empty the contents of several gel packets into the holder before your run, and squeeze out as much gel as you wish during your workout. Dispose of the wrappers where they belong—at home, in the recycling bin, or the trash.

you run faster in the next 30 minutes.) If they contain a little protein along with carbs for optimal recovery, that's great, too, but so does the cheaper banana smeared with peanut butter. In other words, there's nothing these bars can do for you that you can't do for yourself by eating regular food.

These days bars are specialized, billing themselves as preworkout energizers or after-workout recovery fuels. So pay attention to labels. Advertising claims are not always accurate, but the label will tell you if bars include protein (good for recovery) or just quick-acting carbs (good for workouts). And try to stick with bars produced by reputable sports manufacturers: Mainstream manufacturers are wise to the fact that

TRAIL MIX

Running on Empty

I never used to be able to eat before running. It started all the way back in high school, when I insisted on being scheduled for the early lunch period so that my stomach would be settled in time for after-school cross-country practice. By the time I hit my twenties, I needed a 5- or 6-hour window without any food before I'd go running.

Or so I'd convinced myself. In hindsight, my stomach was so empty that any food before a run created acidic havoc. It was a vicious cycle, and I became less and less able to tolerate any food before working out. I got away with this self-imposed starvation as long as I was doing shorter runs and racing, but once the marathon distance beckoned, my coach warned me that I was asking for trouble.

"You need to learn how to eat before running," he'd say. "I can't eat before running," I'd reply. "You can't run for hours on end on an empty stomach," he'd argue. "I can't run at all with anything in my stomach," I'd counter. "You especially need to learn how to drink while you're running," he'd say. "Water—wouldn't touch the stuff," I'd reply. And

sports bars are big sellers, so now they produce "sports bars" that are really nothing more than candy bars in active-looking wrappers.

While sports bars have taken the place of meals for many busy athletes, gels remain largely in the workout world, where they belong. (You don't really want your lunch to slide down your throat like a lump of cake frosting, do you?) Gels are an optimal quick-energy boost of glycogen for long workouts. And yes, they do work. For long runs of up to 3 hours or during a marathon, gels can be a wonder. When your runs creep upward of several hours, you'll need more than a couple of gel packets to get by. That's the time to reach for a fig cookie, trail mix, or another solid food.

so we'd go back and forth, until he threatened to physically hold me down and put a bite of bread in my mouth. "All right, all right"—I consented to one bite of bread. He insisted on a sip of water to go with it. I took the smallest sip I could.

Amazingly, I was able to run. No stomach cramps. No side stitches. The next day I took two bites and two sips. Then three. And so on. And I was fine. In fact, I was dumbstruck. During all those years of avoiding food I'd created my own psychological barrier, and then it was gone.

It's an important lesson: Many runners have some sort of issue when it comes to food. They have to have a certain type of food, or they can't possibly have another type. In fact, a lot of these preferences are probably just in

our heads, and then we reinforce them with our restrictive behavior. And while it's not a good idea to change your traditional practices the day of a race, training runs provide a great opportunity for experimenting on yourself.

Once I trained myself to eat before working out, I found I had a lot more energy on my runs. Instead of being fatigued after 45 minutes, I could go on for hours. As time went on, I was able to branch out from bread. These days, I can eat just about anything before my runs. Maybe it's not the most glamorous accomplishment in my running career, but it's nice to know that if I'm asked to go on a run on short notice and I just ate a turkey sandwich, now I can say "Sure, let's go."

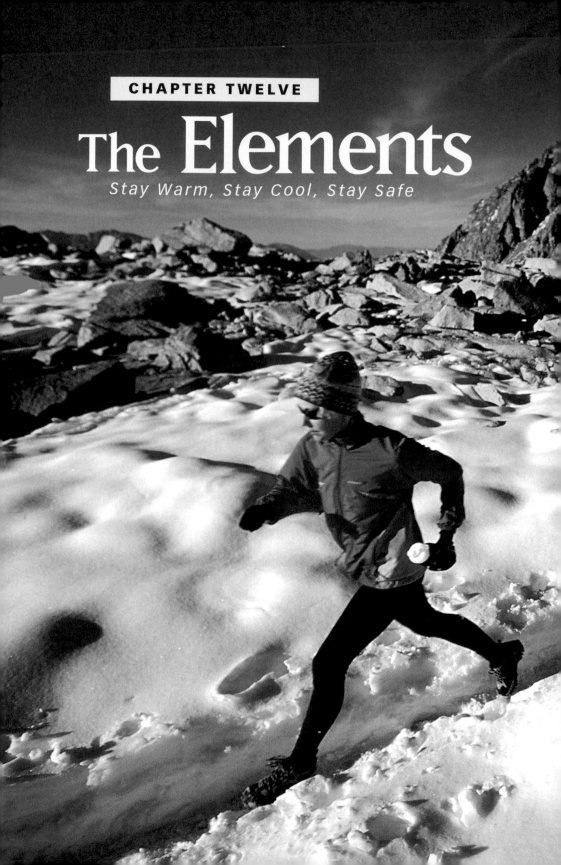

CHAPTER TWELVE

The Elements

Stay Warm, Stay Cool, Stay Safe

Short of a hurricane, the natural world can do little to stop a runner bent on getting his daily dose of miles. Rain? Feels refreshing. Heat? Only bothers sedentary folks. Cold? Heck, running keeps you warm.

More-delicate outdoor athletic endeavors are sometimes canceled because of skin-crawling weather conditions, but you'll almost never see a running race called off when the going gets tough. Mud, rain, snow, heat, wind—they're all part of the game that makes each run a unique challenge.

If you play it smart, you can run safely through most conditions. (Most. Not all. See "hurricanes," above.) On the trail you won't be near covered buildings, well-stocked convenience stores, or telephones, which means you need to be prepared for whatever Mother Nature throws at you—even what you don't expect. Here's how to stay safe, no matter what the weather.

First, Know Yourself

If you remember nothing else about safety, remember this: Know your limits. Sure, everyone is equally vulnerable to certain elements—lightning, for example. But dealing with most other elements is directly related to what you know about your own abilities—both as a runner and a person. And many factors make up those abilities.

For starters, the better your fitness level, the better you'll handle heat and humidity. That's because during exercise, lean bodies with a low percentage of body fat and a well-developed cardiovascular system work less hard and generate less heat.

Acclimatization, the result of gradual exposure to extreme conditions, is another factor in your body's ability to cope outside its optimal operating zone. So if your body is adapted to the heat, for example, it begins to generate sweat sooner and in greater quantities than a nonacclimated one, thus cooling you off more efficiently.

Other adaptive factors are the luck of the draw. Your reaction at high altitude, for example, is somewhat random—some folks are just more susceptible than others, and it has nothing to do with age, gender, fitness, or anything else.

Because so many variables determine how any one person will react in severe conditions, it's important to proceed gradually while you learn how your body will respond to various challenges. If you're setting out in conditions that are new to you, don't be overly ambitious in your running plans. Start slowly and don't expect to cover great distances. Give yourself an "out" by planning routes that allow you to return early if you find you're not tolerating the elements well. Always start off well-hydrated and bring enough water and food for the duration of your run.

Even though they may think they're immune to distress, veteran runners should exercise caution. Hard-core runners are notorious for pushing the limits while uttering disclaimers like "I can run for hours without water" or "Heat doesn't affect me." While they may indeed be more efficient runners in heat or other conditions, they can flout the rules of nature only for so long before falling prey. "There's no physiological way to adapt to a dehydrated state," says Buck Tilton, cofounder of the Wilderness Medicine Institute of National Outdoor Leadership Schools. "You can train your mind to do without water, but not your body." (The body does acclimate and make some adaptations to heat, he notes. For example, as you adapt to heat, you spill fewer electrolytes into your sweat—your sweat is purer, so to speak—so you might feel better and require less in the way of replacement salts. But that's different from saying that you don't require any liquid.)

There's another problem, too. Runners can get so good—and so cocky—that they create problems less fit people would never encounter. "The average runner's build (long and lean) is good for dissipating heat," Tilton says. "And in general, chubby people have heat problems more than lean people." But lean, well-trained athletes are actually prone to serious heat problems during competition or training, he says. "They can push themselves so hard that they literally create heat faster than they can dissipate it." Even the best runners, he cautions, need to know their limits, and eventually that means slowing down, cooling off, and taking a drink.

Running in Heat

A frequent warning during heat waves is to forgo such strenuous activity as, well, running. The first thing runners usually do with such a warning? Ignore it. This is probably not a good idea unless you're very fit. Overweight and untrained runners are more susceptible to heat exhaustion because they work harder during exercise and are less able to dissipate heat. Bluntly put, the leaner and fitter you are, the better you'll cope.

But fitness is a double-edged sword. Well-trained runners are more likely to push themselves to the point of risk precisely because they're so fit. The bottom line is that all runners are susceptible to heat exhaustion and dehydration. The two conditions are closely linked. Dehydration is more of a risk in hotter temperatures because the body loses more fluid through sweat in its attempt to cool itself. In turn, when you're extremely dehydrated, your ability to sweat properly decreases, which compromises your body's cooling system, putting you at greater risk of cramps, heat exhaustion, and heatstroke. Being able to recognize the signs of dehydration and heat illness is vital.

Heat Cramps

Cramps are an early sign of trouble and are usually the first indication that you're overheated and underwatered. These muscle pains and spasms result from dehydration and electrolyte deficiencies. "When you let yourself become dehydrated, your body starts to make choices about where to send the blood," explains Stephen Rice, M.D., Ph.D., a sports medicine physician and director of the Jersey Shore Sports Medicine Center in Neptune, New Jersey. "The body will keep sending blood to the vital areas—the brain and organs. But the sweating and cooling system will be compromised."

At the first sign of cramping muscles, sip a sports drink or drink some water with a little food. Stop running and massage your muscles. If necessary, proceed by walking only after the cramping subsides. Heat cramps must be taken seriously. They're easy to treat, but if you ignore them and suffer ensuing heat illness, you flirt with far more serious consequences.

Heat Exhaustion

Weakness, faintness, chills, and excessive sweating are the signs of heat exhaustion. You may have a weak pulse and experience nausea or even vomiting. Fainting is possible because excessive fluid loss through sweating ultimately reduces blood volume, thus lowering your blood pressure. Heat exhaustion must be treated immediately—it isn't damaging in and of itself, but if left untreated, it can lead to heatstroke, which can rapidly become life threatening.

At the first signs of heat exhaustion, stop exercising, get out of the heat, and rest. Then rehydrate gradually, preferably with a sports drink that contains electrolytes. If water is plentiful, use it to cool your skin. If you can't keep liquids down (thus making hydration impossible), seek immediate medical attention.

Heatstroke

When you ignore heat exhaustion, heatstroke can occur. When your body suffers excessive fluid losses, it eventually loses the ability to sweat. When this happens, your core temperature rises rapidly, with possible fatal consequences. Unlike heat exhaustion, when your skin will appear pale, moist and cool, during heatstroke, your skin will be dry, hot, and red. Your heart rate may rise dramatically and you may experience disorientation or loss of consciousness.

Runners suffering from heatstroke require immediate medical attention. Treatment for heatstroke is not a long-term proposition, but rather one of life-saving urgency. The victim should be cooled by any means possible, with immersion in water, cold clothes, or ice.

Beating the Heat

All runners should exercise caution—and take precautions—when running in the heat. With a little preparation followed by close monitoring, heat illness can be avoided. Here's a checklist of the basic precautions to follow on every warm-weather run:

☐ **Wear light, loose clothing.** A light-colored shirt reflects the sun's rays and heat better than a bare chest and back.

☐ **Stay hydrated.** It's worth repeating: Be sure you're hydrated before heading out, and then drink regularly during the run. On long runs, drink a sports drink or supplement water with salty snacks to replace electrolytes. Dehydration can take place over the course of days. When exercising regularly in the heat—or when running multiday events—it's very important to hydrate continually.

☐ **Block the sun.** Sunscreen not only protects your skin from damage but also keeps your skin temperature lower by reducing burning and inflammation. Choose a sunscreen intended for sports or labeled water resistant—it will be less likely to melt off with your sweat. You can also buy athletic clothes that contain built-in sunscreen. A brimmed hat will keep the sun off your face.

☐ **Start early or late.** When planning a long run of several hours, avoid the heat of the day by setting out in the early morning, late afternoon, or early evening.

☐ **Seek shade.** Choose routes that are sheltered by trees rather than open to the sun.

☐ **Slow down.** When it's hot and humid, your body has to work harder just to run your regular pace. Alter the expectations of your training runs and don't attempt to run your regular pace when it's very hot.

Desert Running

Running in the desert roughly requires the same precautions as for running in the heat—with no room for error. Since it's an arid environment, rest assured you won't find convenient water sources if you misjudge your drinking requirements. And you won't find handy shade trees when you realize you forgot your sunscreen and have begun to toast like a marshmallow. In short, the desert is unforgiving.

"Dehydration is definitely a big factor in the desert environment," says wilderness survival instructor and avid trail runner Matt Graham. "You need to treat your stomach like a canteen." Graham says he drinks up to three quarts of water before a long run in an arid environment. If that sounds like a lot of sloshing, remember: It's hot. You'll be going slow. It's not like you're setting out for a 10-K through the park.

In the desert it's doubly important to wear a hat that provides ample shade for your face and neck, to wear light layers of clothing, and to wear your sunscreen (and bring extra for a second coat when the first one melts off). You'll also want protective sunglasses to shield your eyes from the sun's glare. If you'll be running in sand, consider purchasing special trail shoes with a fabric skirt around the ankle that keeps out debris. And wear socks intended to keep blisters at bay—double-layer construction works well.

Even with proper precautions, the desert is not the place to run solo. Running with a partner increases your chance of having enough water and other supplies, plus you can monitor each other for symptoms of heat illness.

Running in Cold

When running in the cold, it's important to allow your body to limber up gradually. Cold muscles are at greater risk for pulls and strains. Begin your run with a period of slow jogging, then gradually ease into your desired pace. Recognize that you may not be able to achieve or maintain your usual pace in very cold weather, especially if you attempt a faster workout, such as a tempo run.

You can do steady distance runs safely in all but the coldest

tip of the trail

Invisible Sweat

Runners who travel to desert environments often are happily surprised at the lack of sweat they seem to generate on their runs. Mile after mile can go by, but your shorts and socks still stay miraculously dry. Don't be fooled. You do indeed generate plenty of sweat in dry conditions—the difference is that the sweat evaporates readily because of the lack of humidity. And if you look at those shorts closely, you'll probably notice a crust of white salt—the remnants of the sweat you never saw. So be sure to drink heartily even when running in dry conditions. You are sweating profusely. You just can't feel it.

weather. Dress appropriately for your cold-weather run in layers with multiple functions: wicking fabrics near your body, insulating fabrics in the middle, and water-resistant outer layers.

Runners are still vulnerable to the hazards of low temperature. Even though the exertion of running raises your body temperature significantly, poor planning or miscalculations can leave you at risk for hypothermia or frostbite. Long runs are the most risky to undertake in severe cold, due simply to the duration of time you expose yourself to the elements. Hypothermia and frostbite are the two most common ways the cold can rear its nasty head:

Hypothermia

When the body loses heat faster than it can produce it, hypothermia can set in. Technically, it is diagnosed when your temperature drops below 97°F, but since you won't be running with a thermometer, it's more helpful to know the early signs. Symptoms of hypothermia include shivering and loss of energy. You might stumble excessively or act confused or drunk. If your temperature continues to fall, disorientation and hallucinations can set in. Hypothermia can be fatal if it's allowed to progress.

Hypothermia is particularly sneaky because it can creep up on you even when outdoor temperatures are not extremely low. On a slightly cool or windy day, for example, all it takes is for a sweat-soaked runner to slow down the pace during a long run and stop producing his own excessive body heat. Suddenly the runner is wet and cold—and at risk for hypothermia. Trail runners in particular can be at risk on long runs and races when they stop for a break or misjudge their pace and slow down in the later stages of the run. Inadequate fueling—with either food or drink—can increase the risk of hypothermia.

In the early stages of hypothermia, use whatever is available to warm yourself: dry clothing, blankets, and warm liquids are good options. Fuel your body with food and water so as not to exacerbate fatigue. And try to keep moving around to raise your body temperature.

To prevent hypothermia, choose the proper clothing. Multiple layers (ideally consisting of high-tech fabrics that wick and breathe) can keep wind and rain out and allow perspiration to escape, keeping your body warm and dry. Bring along extra layers even on days when you might not expect to be at risk: cool but not cold spring and fall days, for example, especially if there's a chance of precipitation. A rainproof shell, hat, gloves, and even an extra pair of socks are good lightweight items to include in your pack as a safety precaution. Simply shed layers when you're warm (so that they don't get wet) and replace them when you begin to cool.

Frostbite

This problem typically affects the body's extremities, including the tips of the nose, ears, fingers, and toes. The first signs include tingling and itchy sensations, followed by numbness. The skin, which is literally freezing, will also appear discolored, possibly white, yellow, gray, or purplish. Like hypothermia, frostbite also can sneak up on runners when they think they're generating enough body heat to be immune.

The best protection against frostbite is to wear proper clothing. Be particularly careful in your choice of shoes and socks, gloves, and head covering. Shoes should provide adequate protection against the cold—avoid models with excessive mesh and venting. Socks should be a wool or synthetic blend, ideally one that wicks away moisture. Mittens provide more warmth than gloves, allowing the fingers to work together to maintain their body heat. A wind-blocking liner on top of another pair of gloves or mittens is an effective tool to keep hands warm. Finally, hats with earflaps can help protect the ears. In very cold and windy conditions, a face mask, or balaclava, which covers the entire face with holes for eyes and mouth, may be appropriate. At the first signs of possible frostbite, get indoors and warm as soon as possible. The situation won't get better if you stay out in the cold—if you're already not generating enough body heat during your run to counteract the cold, running longer and harder isn't the answer.

In very cold temperatures you may face an additional risk of what's called "frozen lung." Your lungs don't literally freeze; they become irritated by the cold air you suck down while breathing heavily during a run. It generally occurs only in below-zero temperatures and is easily treated by getting out of the cold. Wearing a bandana or scarf over your mouth and nose in very cold temperatures is usually enough to prevent it.

Running at High Altitude

It's an ineffable joy to run, literally, up a mountain. Mountain running holds a different appeal than backpacking or hiking. There's the feeling of traveling light, of letting your feet carry you unassisted to the top of somewhere and back down in less than a day's time. And of course, the views can be breathtaking. But therein lies the catch. Even the best runners are susceptible to altitude sickness. It's an equal-opportunity affliction: No matter how fit you are, if you go up too fast, you're going to get the spins.

Here's why. The higher the altitude, the lower the oxygen concentration in the air. As a result, you must increase your breathing rate to take in the same amount of oxygen as at sea level. Eventually it becomes impossible to maintain a steady level of oxygenation, so you must slow your physical activity accordingly. Over time the body adapts to higher altitude by producing more red blood cells, which increase its ability to transport oxygen. But this doesn't happen in the few hours most trail runners will be exposed to high altitude—it takes days or even weeks.

Altitude sickness manifests itself first through dizziness and breathlessness. There is no set altitude at which people begin to suffer, but symptoms are more common above 9,000 or 10,000 feet after a quick ascent. Prolonged exposure to high altitudes to which you haven't become acclimated can lead to more serious conditions. For example, fluid accumulation in the lungs, or pulmonary edema, can occur after a bout of ordinary mountain sickness. During ultramarathons in which runners traverse high altitudes without much time to acclimate, doctors perform medical checks to be sure runners aren't beginning to show signs of such problems.

Since age, gender, and fitness don't predict your vulnerability to altitude sickness, you won't know if you're prone to it until you go up high. When symptoms arise, reduce your elevation and level of exertion. This can put an end to your run, leaving you and your partners in the lurch, so try to avoid altitude sickness by planning your runs wisely. If you haven't run at high altitude before, proceed gradually. If you're visiting an area of high elevation where you plan to run above 9,000 feet, allow a day or two for your body to acclimate before you try to run at that elevation. Plan short runs at first—or runs that allow the option of turning around or circling back—to see how your body reacts. And always run with a partner so you can monitor each other. Bear in mind that everyone reacts to altitude differently; one runner in the group may suffer while others are fine. In such a case, you cannot expect the afflicted runner to tough it out. Don't forget to stay well-hydrated, since you lose more fluids at high altitude (and acclimatization suffers when you're dehydrated).

Even if you've run at high altitude before, you'll need to reacclimate every time you return. However, you'll remember how your body

Handle with Care

The wet, the cold, the heat—all are Mother Nature's way of re-minding you who's boss when you're running through her wilder-ness. This might be a good place to pause and remember that while you want to keep yourself safe from those reminders, you also want to keep the wilderness safe from you. Bear these guidelines in mind:

STAY ON THE TRAIL. Don't carve your own path, especially in steep areas or places with sensitive soil. You may think it's no big deal to create a shortcut around a bend or take a few steps around the marked trail in search of better footing, but going off the trail can hasten erosion by dislodging rocks, soil, and vegetation. And your footprints may invite others to follow, resulting in further degradation.

Along similar lines, don't take it upon yourself to alter the trail by cutting a wider path or harming vegetation in any way. If a trail you run often is overgrown and needs improvement, and you wish to help, find out which organization oversees the trail and offer your assis-tance for trail renovation. Then follow its guidelines closely. Don't be a maverick and blaze your own way.

LEAVE NO TRACE. Never throw garbage on the trail, and that in-cludes things you may think of as natural. In an arid environment, the orange peel you casually toss over your shoulder can take years to de-compose. In that context it becomes litter. And if you have to relieve yourself, do so a few hundred feet away from any water sources. Dig a hole at least 6 inches deep for solid waste, and cover the hole with dirt when you are finished. If you use toilet paper, pack it out in the plastic bag you brought it in.

SHUT THE DOOR BEHIND YOU. Close cattle gates or similar fencing whenever you pass through.

reacted, so you'll know what to expect the next time. And runners who live at high altitude will find that their bodies do adapt eventually and are better able to process the limited oxygen available.

Running in Storms

In case heat and cold aren't enough, runners have plenty of storm hazards to watch out for as well. They vary in severity—from mild annoyances to severe dangers.

Rain and Hail

Rain is more nuisance than danger on a short run. You'll be home soon enough to change out of your wet gear. On a long run, however, soaked clothes become an invitation to hypothermia on all but the hottest days. That's why it's so important to plan carefully for long runs. Whenever rain is forecast, pack a rain shell, an extra underlayer, a hat, and gloves. If you do get wet unexpectedly in cool conditions, curtail your run and head back. If you feel yourself getting chilled, pick up your pace to generate body heat.

Hail also falls into the nuisance category for the most part. Hailstorms typically are brief affairs (unless you're in the mountains), which means that if you start getting pelted on a run, you can seek cover and wait out the storm. If the hail is small, you may be able to run through it, although even tiny hail pellets can pack a surprising sting. When it's freakishly large—think golf balls or plums—find a tree or rock to hide under and enjoy the show until it's over. Once again, this is a time you'll want to pull out your emergency layers of clothing, since your body temperature will drop once you stop running.

Electrical Storms

Lightning is a risk whenever thunderstorms occur. That means even if you can't see lightning, it might be nearby when you hear thunder. Conventional wisdom tells us to seek shelter when lightning strikes, but you're not likely to find much shelter when you're running on a trail. Your best bet is to move away from trees or other tall objects, such as telephone poles, which attract lightning. Seek out a low, open area, such as a ravine or depression. Crouch down so you're not the tallest thing in your surroundings—squatting is preferable to lying flat, since you're a smaller target that way. And if you have a pack with you, squat on it to insulate yourself from electricity traveling through the ground.

Tornadoes

Unlike hurricanes—for which you get days of warning on the television and radio and have nobody but yourself to blame should you find yourself in the middle of one—tornadoes pretty much happen out of the blue. While they are most common in the American Midwest's "Tornado Alley," they can and do happen elsewhere when conditions are right.

If you find yourself face to face with a tornado, don't attempt to outrun it. No matter how good a runner you are, you're no match for a storm of this nature. If you're not near any sturdy buildings, find a strong structure (a bridge might do) to crouch beside. If none is available, lie flat in a ditch, crevice, or another low area and wait out the storm.

CHAPTER THIRTEEN

Running into Trouble

Bears, Bugs, and Stumbles

The trails you run on typically are probably about as wild and woolly as a Chihuahua puppy. In all likelihood, most days will find you running on gently sloping affairs that would never threaten your ankles, challenge your wits, or meander too far from civilization. You run these everyday trails knowing that if you get low on water, you can cut across a side route and hit the convenience-store cooler.

Of course, other trail runs take you away from these safer confines and lead you smack into wilderness. Some lucky runners live near wilder places and get to enjoy such trails every day. Other runners have to drive to them on the weekends, or perhaps run them while vacationing in the mountains. Whenever you have the chance to head into true wilderness, it's worth it—all the other less spectacular miles you've run will pay off when you find yourself able to run far enough and well enough to get to some wilder places. When you do start going higher up and deeper in, you'll need to expand your knowledge of conventional running safety to include some wilderness common sense and precautions.

Trail runners can get into trouble when they're not aware of hazards or when they fail to heed warning signs. Sure, bad luck is sometimes at play: You can do everything right and still find yourself in a nasty spot. But you can greatly minimize hazards by researching the terrain you'll be traveling, paying attention while you're there, and treating the trail with respect. When you run on a wilderness trail, you're a visitor to a world that belongs to snakes and sun, rocks and trees.

"We always need to treat the wilderness with respect," says Renee Despres, an avid trail runner and wilderness emergency medical technician who has seen the results of foolish behavior. "I want people to trail run, but I want them to do it safely so I don't have to go find them in the middle of the night," she says.

Frequent trail runners should consider taking a wilderness first-aid course, Despres advises. "You'll learn how to take care of yourself in the woods and use the things like sticks and stones that are around." It's a wise idea for anyone spending considerable time on the trail. "If you're serious about running trails, your best first-aid kit is in your head," she says.

This chapter should give you the tools you need to deal with the most common trail hazards. It is based on the collective advice of several wilderness experts, primarily Buck Tilton, cofounder of the Wilderness Medicine Institute of National Outdoor Leadership Schools; Matt Graham, an expert trail runner and field instructor with the Boulder Outdoor Survival School; and the aforementioned Despres.

This information is no substitute for learning everything you can about the trails in your area. Stay apprised of local situations by reading the local newspaper, talking with other trail runners, and checking in with ranger stations or other representatives on forest service land and other publicly held areas. Depending on where you live and run, you may learn of drought or flood that impacts trails, or of animal behavior that should keep you away from certain stretches of trail.

Encountering Wild Animals

Runners fall into two groups: Those who feel it's a rare treat when they spy wild animals on the trail, and those who are terrified at the very idea of encountering anything with teeth or scales. The frightened ones tend to be newer to the trail. Over time and with exposure, humans generally come to learn that most animals are sensible sorts that want nothing to do with people. If we leave the critters alone, chances are they'll do the same. Here's a look at animals most commonly encountered.

Snakes

"Snakes are not a big risk for trail runners," says Tilton. "If you step on one, sure, then it's a risk. But unless the snake is threatened in some way—handled or cornered—they just don't bite. They don't have any natural reason to." So, don't bother them and they won't bother you.

(Tilton jokes that the typical profile of a snakebite victim is "young, male, and intoxicated." Women, he adds, are seldom bitten: "They're a lot smarter.")

Still, snakes do enjoy lounging on the trail and soaking up the sun's rays, making them a seemingly visible threat. But that's the point exactly:

A River Runs through It

Most wilderness wouldn't be wild without some form of water. Most trails will have footbridges or some sort of makeshift crossing—a fallen tree, for example—at the point where they encounter streams and rivers. But water runoff is unpredictable, and sometimes streams will run high, so you may be forced to, well, get your feet wet. Here are a few pointers for safe water crossings:

▲ If stepping-stones or planks have been placed to help people across the water, try to use them. Look for dry spots to step on: You'll have more traction there.

▲ If there are no such aids, look for the shallowest spot possible to cross on your own: You'll see ripples and rocks underneath, whereas the deeper sections of water will appear smooth.

▲ Check downstream first to make sure you're not attempting to cross above a dangerous section of rapids or a waterfall. (If you are, go farther upstream and away from the hazardous section.)

▲ Grab a strong branch, if available, and use it to anchor yourself while walking.

▲ Always face upstream, using your legs to brace you against the current of the water.

▲ Don't take off your shoes. Rocks on the bottom could be sharp and will likely be slippery. You're better off with the traction from your soles.

If you see one, you should be able to avoid it. And if one is hidden nearby and you can't see it, it shouldn't pose a risk.

If you see a snake on the trail, go around it, giving it a wide berth. Most snakes will feel you coming—you're not as light on your feet as you might think—before you even see them and will slither away without incident. And rattlesnakes sometimes give you audible warning, rattling when you are still far enough away to avoid them.

While snake venom is a powerful poison, hardly anyone dies from snakebite in North America. The venom is most dangerous to the elderly, the young, and those in poor health. The potential for harm also depends on where the snake bites you: The closer to your vital organs, the more dangerous it is.

In the unlikely event of snakebite, the goal is to keep venom circulation to a minimum. That means you should stop running, give yourself a few minutes to cool down, and then slowly walk out to seek medical attention, minimizing movement where you've been bitten. Keep the bitten extremity below the level of the heart, if possible. If the bite is on your hand, remove any rings or watches, since swelling is likely. Do not take pain relievers: Pain is the best indication of how much venom has been deposited. Also, some pain relievers act as blood thinners and can therefore speed circulation, perhaps enhancing the effects of the venom. Do not apply a tourniquet, cut or suck on the wound, or apply ice.

Bears

For the most part, bears have no interest in you. The type of bears runners have the best chance of seeing are black bears, which are common throughout the mountain regions of the United States but can also be found in subalpine grassland and forest. Bears begin hibernating in late fall (typically October or November) and continue through the winter for 3 to 6 months. In spring and summer they actively stock up on food to get them through their next long sleep. Cubs are often seen with their mothers in late spring and summer.

"Bear become more problematic around people and camp-grounds," Graham points out. "In those settings they see people as more vulnerable and start to test people's limits. Bear will grab food out of people's hands in a campground setting, but the further you get out into the wilderness, the fewer problems you'll have." While the bear's diet does include small mammals and fish, along with berries and clover, a human being doesn't exactly fit into its typical menu. Put another way, you are more of a curiosity than a meal source. Still, you don't want to provoke a bear: They have been known to charge, particularly females that perceive a threat to their cubs.

Should you run across a bear, it will most likely be scared of you and leave the scene. If the bear stands its ground, back away slowly to give it space and head to other environs. Give the bear every opportunity to avoid you—bears rarely attack, and usually once you (the threat) disappear, so does the bear. Try talking to it in a normal voice—this will help the bear establish that you are human and therefore not a threat. Bears sometimes engage in bluff charges, in which the bear will stop short several yards away. If a bear comes at you, stand your ground. Don't run, as it might give chase. In the very unlikely event of an attack, curl into a ball and "play dead." Typically, the bear will cease the attack once it thinks any threat is gone. In the rare event that the bear continues its aggression after you've tried to play dead, it's time to fight back vigorously in any manner possible, including hitting or using a stick or rock.

Mountain Lions

Mountain lions (also known as pumas, cougars, and panthers) are most commonly seen in mountainous regions of the western United States. Because they're predators, they're more problematic than other animals in the wild. "Most animals are more afraid of you than you are of them, unless it's a lion—a lion can sometimes be looking for lunch," Despres says.

A few trail runners have been attacked by lions. But despite the headlines such incidents generate, the risk of a mountain lion encounter is exceedingly small. Tilton points out that invariably, runners or hikers who have been attacked by lions were traveling alone, and were therefore seen by the lion as more vulnerable. Running with a partner greatly decreases your likelihood of even seeing a lion.

If you do see a lion, stop. "Running is what prey does, and it triggers the chase instinct," says Despres. To seem less like prey, make it as clear as possible that you are a large, strong human: Stay in an erect posture and hold your hands up over your head to appear bigger. Speak in a human voice; do not growl or attempt to make any animal-like noises. And avoid direct, deep eye contact, which the lion may perceive as threatening. Meanwhile, back away slowly while continuing to face the animal.

Insects

Most of the bugs you encounter while running can be classified as more of an annoyance than an outright danger. Gnats congregate near lakes and ponds, clouding the trail in summer months intent on suicide missions that end in one of your eyes. Horseflies, deerflies, and the like seem to have no trouble keeping pace with runners, their nips and bites a familiar nuisance in some parts of the country. They don't present any real danger but they can make a run less pleasant. If irritation lingers after a run, apply an anti-itch ointment (usually containing an analgesic, antihistamine, corticosteroid, or some combination of the three).

More serious are bee, wasp, or hornet stings. People who are allergic are at risk for anaphylaxis, a potentially life-threatening allergic reaction during which breathing passageways can shut down and the heart can cease to beat normally. Anaphylaxis is an emergency requiring immediate treatment, typically an injection of epinephrine. If you know you are allergic to insect stings, always carry an EpiPen (a syringe of epinephrine). If you ever need to inject yourself with epinephrine in the wake of a sting, seek follow-up care with a doctor. Because your first exposure to a bee sting may not trigger an allergic reaction, you may be allergic and not know it. If you have had a strong reaction to stings in the past, consult with your doctor about the possibility that you are allergic and should take precautionary measures.

If mosquitoes are common where you run, it's a good idea to wear bug repellent. Once considered just a nuisance, they have become a more serious threat because of mosquito-borne illnesses, such as the potentially fatal West Nile virus. Ticks, fleas, and chiggers can spread Lyme disease, Rocky Mountain spotted fever, or other ailments. These parasites are most prevalent in wooded, shady areas, especially near open fields. If you run in these areas, wear insect repellent. Also examine your body after your workout. Should you find a tick attached to your skin, carefully remove it—head and all—with tweezers. It's generally thought that the tick must be in contact with your body for several hours in order to transmit disease, so time is on your side. If you're out running all day, stop every few hours to examine yourself.

Scorpions and Spiders

Scorpions are found in desert and subtropical areas, but they are nocturnal, making encounters rare for runners. (Backpackers are a more usual target—it's not uncommon for the critters to take up residence in a warm hiking boot overnight.) Still, if you suspect you've been stung, seek medical attention. Scorpion stings are most dangerous to children, the elderly, and people with compromised immune systems.

Spiders are also reclusive, meaning their bites are easily avoided by staying on the trail. Since spiders typically wait for their prey to come to them, bushwhacking through the brush is a trail runner's best invitation to a spider bite. The most common poisonous spiders in the United States are of the widow family—small, dark spiders with the telltale hourglass marker on their abdomens—and the brown recluse (or fiddleback) spider, which has a violin-shaped mark on its back. If you suspect a spider has bitten you, seek medical treatment.

Finally, be respectful of all the creatures you encounter. "Although it's the large animals that get the press, most of the real dangers you're going to face in the woods come from smaller or less glamorous things like insect bites," says Despres. For example, skunks, squirrels, and other rodents carry rabies. If one is acting aggressive or stumbling around looking injured, stay away from it, she advises. Moose and bison have been known to attack if they feel threatened, especially during rutting season (generally September and October). If you encounter one of these animals, simply run the other way. As herbivores, they won't give chase.

Avoiding Poisonous Plants

Poisonous plants generally come in two categories: Those that cause trouble when you touch them and those that cause trouble when you eat them. Runners can keep things simple by never eating any wild plants—this shouldn't be hard to do, as long as you don't forget your sports bars and pretzels. Touching a poisonous plant may be a little harder to avoid on the trail. Poison ivy and poison oak are the two most common plants that cause contact dermatitis, the fancy name for the inflammation, redness, itching, and blistering of the skin that come after exposure. Common throughout North America, poison ivy grows along the ground or climbs like a vine up trees. Poison oak, also found throughout North America, grows like a bush and is therefore more confined. Poison sumac, a tall-growing shrub, can also cause serious contact dermatitis but is less common, found only in wet, swampy areas. If you think you've run into a patch of poisonous vegetation, the best course of treatment is to wash the area of your skin aggressively with soap and water as soon as possible. Also wash any clothes you were wearing. If the skin aggravation is intense, see your pharmacist or physician about a corticosteroid cream to relieve symptoms.

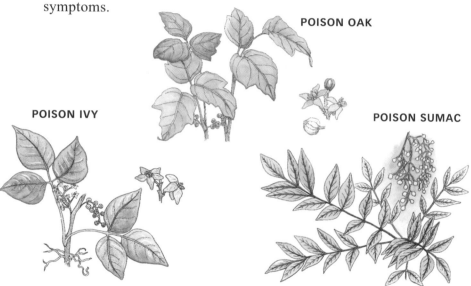

POISON OAK

POISON IVY

POISON SUMAC

Cactus spines, while not poisonous, can also cause irritation and inflammation. The possibility of a cactus encounter is another in a long list of reasons that you should stick to the marked trail. But a fall or even a few steps through the brush is all it takes to wind up with a hand or an ankle full of spines. If you know you're running in cactus country, bring a pair of tweezers in your pack. Use the tweezers immediately to remove as many of the spines as possible. If you don't have tweezers on hand, you can try using your teeth or a pair of pliers when you get back to your car. Remove the spines gently—some types break off easily—tugging in the same direction they entered, as you would with a splinter.

Staying Away from Hunters

Hunting seasons vary depending on where you live, but generally they run from autumn to early spring. While most veteran hunters pose little danger to runners, accidents do happen, so it's always a good idea to take some precautions during hunting season. Runners should:

- Know when and where hunting is allowed.

- Wear bright colors, preferably the blazing orange that hunters favor, to stand out from the muted colors of nature.

- Run in groups whenever possible. And if you're with a partner, it doesn't hurt to talk loudly during your runs.

Wearing bright clothing makes you more visible to (and safer from) hunters.

▲ Stay on the trail. You shouldn't be running off the trail anyway, but especially not during hunting season.

▲ Consider another route. If you find your favorite trailhead filled with trucks containing empty gun racks, run elsewhere.

Follow these rules even if you're running through areas where hunting is not allowed: Hunters who break the law and go into areas that are off-limits can still pose a risk.

Dealing with Acute Injuries

The upside of trail running is that you're less likely than a road runner to suffer repetitive use injuries such as stress fractures or plantar fasciitis. The downside is that you are more likely to suffer sudden injuries, such as the dreaded ankle roll or torqued knee. Injuries of this nature are not really a matter of "if," but "when" and "how bad." If you run long enough, you'll trip, or twist, or stumble, or do something that brings your run to an abrupt halt.

Most of these injuries aren't life threatening, but they can make it tricky to get back to your starting point. As Tilton says, "you're not going to chop an arm off trail running." The most common trail running injuries are skin abrasions from falls, and twisted ankles and knees. Sprained wrists and broken bones are a rare occurrence. "One of the smarter things a runner can do is to learn to tape their own ankle," Tilton says. And to keep drinking. Dehydration and heat illness, while not technically injuries, are actually a far greater risk to runners than most other problems combined. (For more on heat illness, see chapter 12.)

Any first aid you perform on the trail should simply minimize further harm before you can seek proper medical attention. "If you can walk out, then do it—that's the fastest way to get medical help," says Despres. If you are incapacitated, that's where having a running buddy or having somebody know where you're running comes into play."

Here's a look at trailside first-aid treatment for some of the most common injuries you might sustain during a run.

Ankle Rolls

You can tell right away just how serious a twisted ankle is by how much it hurts. Some very dramatic ankle rolls that seem serious while they're happening may do very little damage—it all depends on the way your foot twists. If you got away easy, mild discomfort will be the only manifestation, and you may even be able to keep running, or at least walking. Severe twists that damage ligaments are not only very painful, but they also require some immobilization. "If there's any way to do so, you'll still want to try to walk out," Despres points out. "But try to reduce the motion of the injured leg as much as possible. It's what you'll want to do anyway, to reduce the pain." Despres

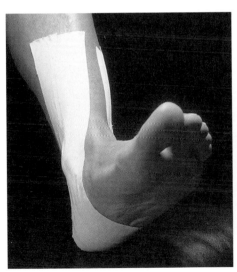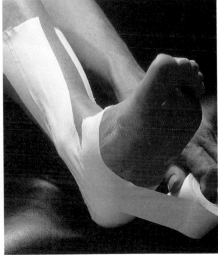

When taping an ankle, run a few long pieces down one side, under your foot, and up the other side, to discourage lateral movement. Then anchor it with additional pieces of tape crisscrossing around the front and back of the ankle, again running them under the foot for stability.

recommends looking around you for tools. "You can use a stick for a makeshift crutch. Or get creative and find something to splint it against. If you're carrying athletic tape, you can tape it as well." The idea is to keep the injured ankle from moving around and still walk out to civilization.

Once you're back home, seek medical attention for serious sprains. Otherwise, treat your ankle as soon as possible with rest, ice, compression, and elevation (or RICE therapy). Rest the injury by getting off your feet. Ice the area immediately, and continue icing a few times a day for the next few days. Compress the ankle with an elastic bandage, and keep it elevated.

Cramps

Two kinds of cramping typically afflict runners: muscle cramps and digestive cramps. If you develop muscle cramps during your run, chances are you're dehydrated and in the early stages of heat illness. Never ignore muscle cramps: They're an early indicator of bigger troubles ahead and are easily treated—heatstroke (the eventual result of untreated heat illness) is not. At the first sign of cramps, decrease your exertion by slowing to a walk or stopping. Swallow water or a sports drink and eat some pretzels or other food to boost your electrolytes. If you have extra water, pour some over your head and body to cool down. Massaging your muscles will ease the cramps, but cooling off and hydrating are more effective in treating the cause of the cramps and preventing further problems. (For more on heat illness, see chapter 12.)

Digestive cramping is most likely to occur during ultramarathon competitions or long-duration training runs. When suffering stomach or bowel distress, reduce your pace or walk. Slowly sip fluids, since dehydration could be the cause. Eat bland, plain foods to help settle your stomach—pretzels and bread are good choices. When you run for longer than several hours, training your stomach to tolerate the necessary food to fuel your run is just as important as any other training you do. Try various foods on runs of moderate distances to determine the best types of fuel for you. (For more on eating on the run, see chapter 11.)

Cuts and Wounds

Surface injuries can range from annoying scrapes that are little more than road rash to deep cuts that will eventually require stitches. In most cases, a little blood won't require you to stop your run. However, depending on the seriousness and the location of the wound, other cuts might need immediate attention. In the case of surface wounds, bleeding is the real danger, so your first concern should be to stop it. Apply di-

Out of Joint

Some trail runners can develop a propensity for twisting their ankles. "Once you strain the ankle, it can get stretched out, and you run the risk of doing it again—you might go through a stage where you're rolling it over and over," says Douglas Wisoff, a physical therapist who logs hundreds of miles every month on the trails. To prevent such a recurrence, strengthen your ankle and leg areas. Weight exercise, resistance bands, balance boards, and mini-trampolines all can develop balance and musculature in the area to avoid further ankle rolls. Finally, while it's fine to tape an ankle for immediate relief after a strain, it's not a good idea to get into the habit of running with such bracing. Prolonged artificial support can weaken the ankle and leave it more vulnerable to injury in the future.

Blisters and Black Toenails

Runners often complain about these nagging side effects of the sport they love. Blisters and bruised toenails can arise suddenly and make a trail run downright miserable. Your best strategy against either of these problems is prevention: Choose smooth socks that don't rub at the seams and are made of synthetic materials that wick away moisture. Wear shoes that fit—most damaged toenails result from having a toe jamming against the front of the shoe when running downhill. There should be about a half-inch of space between your longest toe and the shoe. And keep your toenails trimmed short.

Even with precaution, blisters do happen. When you return home, wash the area well. Try to leave the skin covering intact whenever possible; that way, infection is less likely. A very full blister that is too painful to walk on can be drained carefully (pop it with a sterile pin), but be sure to keep the area clean and washed afterward. You can try a synthetic-skin bandage that provides protection from infection, but the blister should also heal just fine on its own. Meanwhile, avoid wearing the shoes that caused the blister, so that you don't keep aggravating the same hot spots.

Black toenails are the result of blood blisters under the nail. Because of their inaccessible location, there's little you can do to treat them. Keep an eye on them to be sure they don't get infected. If they do, you'll need to see a podiatrist. It's not unusual for a blackened toenail to eventually "die" and fall off. It's certainly not a pretty sight, but it's also not dangerous. In most cases, a new nail will grow in its place.

rect pressure to the wound or to the artery just above it. If possible, elevate the afflicted area above heart level to further slow the bleeding. You may have to do this for several minutes before bleeding slows or stops. Once you return home, clean the wound with water and an antiseptic soap. If the wound is deeper than a half-inch or gapes open, seek professional medical care.

A word about tourniquets: According to Despres, your hand—not a tourniquet—is the best tool for applying pressure. If you cut off your circulation with such a device, you risk losing a limb. Tourniquets also make infection more likely.

Head Injuries

As with other injuries, you should try to keep walking after hitting your head during a fall. "It's true that people with certain injuries

First Aid to Go

Obviously, carrying an entire medicine cabinet's contents while running is impractical. But it's not a bad idea to carry an abbreviated first-aid kit, especially for long runs or runs that take you to remote areas. You don't even have to put one together from scratch—outdoors stores sell small, lightweight kits outfitted with the basics for just this purpose. Buy one and stash it permanently in your pack. You won't even notice it—until you need it, and then you'll be glad you have it. You can supplement the kits with a few other handy items, such as a roll of athletic tape and a pair of tweezers.

Staying Found

It's rare to get deeply lost while trail running. After all, it's not called off-trail running. Or thwacking-your-way-through-the-bushes-with-no-idea-where-you're-going running. You're following a trail. Or you're supposed to be, anyway.

Still, you need to pay a little more attention on the trail than if you were cruising around in circles at the local track. While some trails are veritable superhighways, others are stingy paths with little in the way of marking. Still others have so many turnoffs and spurs that it's tough to decide which path is the one you want. So it is possible to find yourself running a few extra miles you never intended to cover.

How to avoid these unplanned detours? Staying found on a trail is largely a matter of paying attention. Stay focused on your surroundings. Here are a few tips on navigating the way:

HAVE AN OVERALL SENSE OF THE DIRECTION YOU'RE HEADED. If you're doing an out-and-back run, find something big that you can rely on as a landmark, such as the mountains, the ocean, or the sun. That way you'll know that if on the outbound trip, for example, the mountains are on your left, they should be on your right on the way back. The same thing applies if you're doing a loop: You should have a general sense of whether you're headed in the right direction. I'm talking about the broadest, general terms here—basically knowing whether you're heading north, south, east, or west.

HAVE A SENSE OF THE SMALLER LANDMARKS YOU PASS. As you run, pick out memorable landmarks: A very distinctive tree, a rock formation, a lake. On the way back, passing these points will ensure you are on the right path.

PAY ATTENTION ANY TIME YOU REACH A CROSSROADS. Following a trail is easy. It's when the trail splits that you can make mistakes in navigation. Sometimes runners get into trouble because things look different on the way back than they did on the outbound trip. When you come to a crossing, turn around and view the crossing from the direction you'll see it on the way back. Remember this view, and make mental notes to help you remember the path you need to choose.

DO RESEARCH AHEAD OF TIME. Look at a map and talk to other runners before running an unfamiliar trail. This is especially important with loop trails that are not clearly marked. Because you won't be returning over the same ground, you won't have confirmation that you're going the correct way. If you're on a loop course, try to learn which other trails may cross yours—then you'll know what to look for, and you'll be better able to stay on your course. If a map is available, bring it with you on your run.

RUN WITH A PARTNER IN UNFAMILIAR TERRITORY. If you want to check out a new trail, go with a group or a partner, preferably someone familiar with the trail. Companions can point out any tricky spots, as well as points of interest. Only when you're certain you know where you're going should you go it alone.

STAY PUT. If you ever do become truly lost while on a long run in the backcountry, rule number one is to stay put. The worst thing you can do when lost in the wilderness is to keep wandering. That's because if you move around, odds are you'll move farther away from your original route. By staying close to your planned route, you increase your chance of rescue. The moment you think you may be lost, the best thing to do is stop. Sit down and stay calm. Don't let panic drive you deeper into the unknown. If you took proper precautions—telling a friend or family member where you would be running ahead of time—you'll become found soon enough.

shouldn't be moved except by professionals," Tilton says. Generally, you should remain immobile after any injury that causes difficulty breathing or that might have involved the brain. "But there's the practical question—where are you? If you think you have a serious head injury but it will be a few days before someone will walk by, you should try to walk out. You might have no other choice." And of course, seek medical attention from a physician as soon as possible.

After sustaining a head injury, stay away from nonsteroidal anti-inflammatory drugs (NSAIDs), which include aspirin and ibuprofen. A blow to the head can cause internal bleeding, which these drugs can exacerbate because they thin the blood and impair its ability to clot. All pain relievers, including acetaminophen (Tylenol), should be avoided for the first 24 hours after a head injury, since they interfere with your ability to monitor pain and evaluate your injury.

Fractures

If you suspect you have broken a bone, try to immobilize the area. You may have to get creative: Look around for sticks or other makeshift splints, and use athletic tape or your clothing to tie the area to the splint. A sturdy branch can function as a crutch to take weight off a leg or ankle. Any immobilization will help the pain— even holding your arm with your hand, for example, is better than nothing. As with the other injuries mentioned above, your goal should be to walk out whenever possible and get immediate medical attention.

Avoiding Crime

No matter how far away from civilization you run, crime remains a fact of life. Fortunately, most trailside crime occurs right at the trailhead and falls under the category of theft—aggravating, to be sure, but no personal harm done. An unlocked car at a trailhead is an easy target, as is any car with valuables left in sight. To lessen the likelihood of theft, lock wallets, bags, purses, radios, and any other obvious items of value in the trunk. And, of course, lock the rest of the car. Don't hide your keys in the wheel well or under the bumper, a practice common among many runners.

More serious crime does occur on the trails, of course, although it's not common. Assaults and abductions have taken place in the most remote and seemingly idyllic of places. For most runners, this is just a cautionary fact of life: A rare and unlikely circumstance to take note of, but certainly not a factor that should stop someone from running on trails.

It does make sense to be smart about crime even on trails: Try to always run with a buddy. If you run alone, tell someone where you plan to go and how long you intend to be gone. And heed local events and warnings. If crime has been noted in an area you frequent on your runs, stay away until it has been deemed safe by authorities.

TRAIL MIX

Turf Wars

What is it about people and snakes? With each snake encounter of my own I become more convinced that these serpents have far more to fear from us than we from them.

A few years back I was running along a trail quite close to home when I came across a man wielding a huge branch. "Watch out!" he cried. "There's a snake here!" And indeed there was, a large rattler smack in the middle of the trail, coiled and agitated.

"Well, just leave it and go around," I replied. I assumed he had been trying to pick it up with the branch in order to relocate it off the trail.

"No—it's going to bite!"

"Well, yeah—because you've been trying to move it."

"No, I'm trying to get rid of it." And with that, he smacked the branch down on top of the snake. I was stunned.

"What are you doing?!" I yelled. "Just leave it!" He ignored me, intent on his mission. I was close to the end of my run and had limited energy—and was also questioning the wisdom of entering into an altercation with a man

already hitting things—so I decided to exit the situation, simply jogging to the side of the trail, running wide by several yards, and leaving the snake and its attacker behind.

I couldn't—and still don't—understand why he didn't just go around the snake himself. Some people must believe snakes have superpowers, possessing the ability to jump and strike yards away from where they lie. Perhaps these people are afraid to go around, figuring a snake can stalk and bite them no matter how wide a berth they give it.

But after my most recent encounter, I've come to believe that some folks just relish the fight. I was running with a friend on another trail when we came upon a man who had stopped in a wide, rocky clearing.

"There's a snake over here," he warned, pointing off to the side of the trail. Seeing nothing, my friend and I kept running.

"Just leave it," I said as we passed. "Just go around and you'll be fine."

As we ran on, I felt a little guilty.

"There you go bossing people around again," I thought. But since I had just been researching and writing this very chapter, and had been discussing with experts how to handle snakes, it had just popped out of my mouth. We ran on, soon forgetting the encounter.

On our return, as we approached the same spot on the trail, we saw the same man. More than an hour had passed, and he wasn't 50 yards from where we'd originally seen him. My friend and I wondered what he had been up to. "Now I really am scared," I joked, "if he's been messing with that snake this whole time, we probably will get bit!"

It turns out we had nothing to fear. Another few yards down the trail we saw the result of his handiwork: a dead rattler on the edge of the trail, bloodied, with its head smashed. We stopped, shocked. "He killed it. I can't believe he killed it." We stood there just staring. And then, I confess, I yelled back in his direction, "You [use your imagination here]!"

Now I really felt guilty—instead of feeling bad for being bossy, I felt shamed that I hadn't done enough. Should we have done something differently? We had told him to leave the creature alone.

Could we have known that this yahoo would feel the need to bludgeon a snake that posed him no harm?

And what should I do next time I run across someone harassing a snake? Physically shove him away down the trail? Not a realistic possibility. But I have had enough creepy human encounters to learn a lesson. Next time I run across a person threatening a snake, I hope I'll have the courage to take a minute out of my run. Maybe I'll try to explain how snakes "think" and why they're not a threat if you just leave them alone. Maybe I'll explain why it's not okay to harass and even kill them on their own turf—because, after all, the trail is their turf. Runners, hikers, cyclists—and any other yahoos—are just passing through. Let's never forget that.

As my friend and I finished our run home, I remembered Buck Tilton's words about most snakebite victims being "young, male, and intoxicated." This guy was at least two out of three. I secretly hoped that snake had gotten its hooks into his young, male butt before it met its demise. But I also knew it probably wasn't the case. As I thought about it, that guy looked far too happy and satisfied walking away.

CHAPTER FOURTEEN

Our Bodies, Our Brains

The Mental Side of Running

Yogi Berra once said that baseball is 90 percent mental and the other half is physical. The same goes for running. In other words, to be a successful runner, you can't have one aspect without the other. In order to do the type of training required to push your limits, you must be mentally tough. On the flip side, mental toughness is worthless if you haven't done the physical work required to prepare your body for the task at hand.

When runners become interested in more than recreational fitness and begin racing for speed or running ultra distances, the sport turns into a different beast. At its toughest, running is very simply about overcoming discomfort. Few other sports are so clearly a matter of seeing how much you can push your body. Other sports rely more on accuracy, teamwork, balance, and coordination. But running becomes a blunt matter of lifting your legs up and putting them down again no matter how much it hurts.

Running Tough

The mental aspect of pain management can be learned, although some people seem naturally better at it than others. Indeed, the competitive side of the sport seems to attract people enticed by pushing themselves to see how much punishment they can take. These runners enjoy the idea of running around the edges of possibility. For others, that's a less pleasant, more daunting concept. Runners considered mentally tough draw their strength from different sources, but most have a few talents and characteristics in common.

A Positive Focus

Self-talk is a powerful motivator—and also a powerful source of defeat. If you tell yourself you can't do something, your body will listen. If your mind says, "I'll never get up that hill," then you won't. It's critical to keep your thoughts positive to convince your body that your goals are indeed possible. Next time you find yourself saying "I can't" while you're running, change your thinking process. Focus on positive affirmations, such as: "This hill is a challenge, but that's what I love about this sport. I've trained for this, and I know I can do it."

An Ability to Manage the Unmanageable

At many points in a race or long run, the task at hand can seem unimaginable. At the start of a long run that's to last several hours, or even in a 10-K during which you plan to run a daunting pace for the whole race, it can seem downright impossible. Thinking of your run in these grand terms can be self-defeating.

Instead, break down your race or run ahead of time and have a well-conceived, realistic plan of action. Then, once you actually start the run, it's more helpful to only think of where you are in the moment. Instead of thinking, "I have 25 miles to go," concentrate on finishing the mile you're currently running. Rather than worrying how you'll feel many hours from now, get yourself through the hour. When things get really tough, you may need to break it down even more. In the latter stages of a competition, keep your mind on just getting to the top of the next hill, or just relaxing for the next flat stretch until around the bend. Don't mistake this with a form of denial—actually, you're keeping your mind from working against you. After all, you always know you can run just 1 more mile, or just 5 more minutes, or even just 10 more steps. And then 10 more. And then 10 more.

Intense Concentration

If you're not interested in running fast, one of the best ways to get through the painful parts of a workout is to tune out. Long runs can be much more enjoyable if you're gazing at the daisies or composing shopping lists in your head—sometimes you can even forget you're working. If you disassociate in this way, you'll feel better, but you'll also slow down. It requires tremendous concentration to maintain a fast pace or a high level of effort once it begins to hurt. To maintain your effort, for better or for worse, you've got to stay present and work through the hurt. Some runners will create a mantra of sorts, repeating it over and over to themselves—"I'm okay; keep it up; doing great"—to stay focused on the task at hand.

No Fear of Pain

If you run long and hard enough, it will hurt. That's a given. If you're afraid of hitting this point, you'll never be able to run to your fullest potential. You can approach pain with fear and revulsion, or you can approach it matter-of-factly. In the latter stages of a race, when you're suffering from a buildup of lactic acid or you're simply sore and tired, try to be objective about it. Avoid feelings of defeat by telling yourself you knew that this point was coming, and now's the time to be tough. Some runners like to tell themselves the race will be over soon enough and they can rest once they finish what they set out to do. (I'm talking about the normal discomfort that comes with the exertion of running. Never ignore severe pain, acute injury, dehydration, and signs of heat or cold affliction. Ignoring serious problems is not mental toughness; it's just plain stupidity.)

Finding Motivation

Motivation is in more generous supply for trail runners than road runners. After all, what's not to like about taking time out of the day to enjoy the serenity and beauty of a trail? It's a lot easier to gear up for a stroll through nature than to slog some miles through the staccato of traffic lights.

Still, every runner has days when any exercise at all sounds like a grind, and the couch beckons more seductively than the trail. On such days, a few motivational tricks can get your feet off the ground.

Just get started. Don't think about completing that hour-long run you had planned. If you feel tired, just promise yourself to get out the door and try. Jog the first mile slowly—probably you'll warm to the task and feel more energized after you begin.

Remember why you run. If your workout suddenly sounds like a chore, focus on the benefits of running. You're healthier and happier in the long term thanks to running. But even this individual run can make a difference: Each run revs your metabolism, burning calories and building fitness. And a run can be just the thing to improve your mood if you're feeling blue or to give you an energy boost if you're uninspired.

Find a partner. On days when it's hard to get out the door, it can be much easier to run with a friend. You won't want to disappoint a partner who's waiting for you. And conversation can distract you from the run itself—the workout becomes more social event than chore.

Mix up your training. Sometimes it's not really lack of motivation that's getting you down, but boredom with your routine. Don't run the same route every day. Try a new trail. Or instead of doing the same paced distance all the time, do some fartlek runs to play around with your pacing. Or run the uphills hard and the downhills easy. The idea is to bust out of your rut.

Train for a race. Running day in and day out without a goal can be monotonous. Even if you're not a serious competitor, you can enjoy the challenge and camaraderie of a race. More trail races are scheduled every year, at every distance, and covering every type of terrain. By choosing an event and planning for it, you're more likely to get out the door and do the required training.

When you're really tired, give yourself a break. There's a difference between being lazy and being exhausted. Sometimes you truly do need a rest day that you hadn't planned on. If you really are too tired to run, even after you've tried to warm up for a mile or so, call it quits and take the day off. And remember, it's not just your running that can make you tired: Other stresses can take their toll and cut into your running energy. A hard week at work or caring for a sick child can also be cause for a much-needed rest day.

When You Don't Want to Stop

Lack of motivation isn't an issue for everyone. In fact, some runners have no problem getting out the door every day; instead, they're unable to quit. Some people even find that running becomes an addiction. Some prefer to call it a positive addiction; after all, it doesn't have the negative connotations of such unhealthy addictions as tobacco or alcohol. It can be justified, ostensibly, because it is a healthy, life-affirming activity. This means it can also be a very tricky addiction to control.

It's hard to say exactly when enough is enough, and when running becomes a compulsion instead of just a hobby. Some clues are obvious, such as when a runner continues to train even when pain makes walking difficult, or frequently ignores family and social events in order to run.

Because it's possible to run for so long on the trail, trail runners may be more susceptible to such imbalances. If you run on the roads, 2 or 3 hours are the maximum you'll likely be able to run. If you factor in walking breaks and beautiful scenery, a trail runner can justify being gone all day. That's fine—if other aspects of your life remain in balance. But if you're leaving work unfinished or a partner unhappy, it may be time to rethink priorities.

Running, like every other facet of life, should always be kept in perspective. Balance is the key, says Leon Hoffman, Ph.D., a clinical psychologist in private practice in Chicago. Hoffman, a runner himself who has counseled many runners in his practice, has seen running affect marriages and jobs, but he's also seen the good it does his patients. "The idea is not to get carried away with a lust for the activity. Running is a part of a much more important thing. Picture an organizational chart—

running would be like a vice president of manufacturing or something, not the top slot. It should come under the rubric of something bigger." In other words, running should be a means to an end, not the end itself.

Hoffman explains that daily running is not a problem in and of itself; it's the attitude toward the running that can become troublesome. "Routines are important in our life because they reduce anxiety," he says. "But it's important to distinguish between routine and ritual. Rituals get obsessive. And when it becomes a ritual rather than a routine, you have to look at the underlying situation. When running becomes compulsive—when someone doesn't know why they're doing it—the person is acting out."

Compulsive runners can take many forms. Some don't feel "right" unless they run for at least an hour a day. Some insist on running even when they're sick or injured. Still others use running as a calorie-burning obsession, in an attempt to burn off more calories than they consume each day. If you suspect you may be such a runner, try to rethink your goals and seek professional therapeutic help to better understand your behavior and make sure running isn't an escape from a more serious problem. Running should be an enjoyable part of a healthy lifestyle.

CHAPTER FIFTEEN

A Final Note

Wherever the Trail May Lead You

O n the trail you can run away from problems. You can run toward answers. You can lose yourself. You can find peace. And if you run long enough, you will find magic—I'm convinced of it.

The magic we find on the trail can be found both far from home and near. Sometimes it is beautiful to behold, and other times it's more frightening. I've had runs where all of a sudden, born of sweat and breath and exertion, everything in my world seemed startlingly clear. The questions that can hang so heavy and oppressive while I'm shut in at a desk can take on a clarity out on the trail: "Yes, I should move to a new town." "No, I should not take that job." The simplicity of the trail seems to sort everything out. It becomes clear that life is good—or that life has to change.

Since I was a child I've looked for those answers out on the trail. I grew up near the forest preserves of northern Illinois, a dense, deciduous forestland. In my memory, it is always winter. I ran to get away from home. It could be cold enough to freeze the inside of my nostrils with every breath, but still I would run. I'd pick up the trail a mile or so from home, snow crunching underfoot. The trail would grow hard to follow; I would bushwhack through trees and undergrowth.

When I go back now, I realize it isn't that large an area, a few miles from end to end. But there was magic and mystery for a child. I could never remember the trail from the last time I'd run it. Wrong turns made for the best times, anyway. One day I ran into a farm, sheep and horses in their pens. I crept through the snow to get as close as I dared. But on later runs I couldn't find it again, as if it hadn't been real. Other times I would find remains of cabins, with bits and pieces of the lives that inhabited them all those years ago—a pot, a chair. I would imagine living there, in the woods, on the trail. I'd imagine I didn't have to go back home.

I returned a few years ago and ran down to the Des Plaines River, following a tiny trail my brother and I used to take. The wooded expanses of my childhood were now reduced to a sliver of trees and brush, with newly built houses visible on either side. But it was winter, just like I remembered it. As I entered the tangled trail, a brush of russet flashed in front of me: a fox's tail. I stopped. He stopped. He turned around and looked. Then he trotted up ahead, but not in a great hurry. He looked back again, as if to say, "Let's play." I followed his weaving gait for several hundred yards before he turned off the trail as we reached the river.

And there I was once again. Just like when I was a child. I stopped my run and folded myself down onto the snow on the banks of the river. And just like I remembered, as long as I was out here on the trail, everything was okay. For these few minutes in the day, work didn't loom. And my family wasn't so screwed up. And I wasn't tired or worried about anything. For these few minutes, life was simple and beautiful and as crystal clear as the air and frost around me. I sat until my sweat grew cold, until I knew that it was time to go back.

Running in Queensland, Australia, several years ago, I caught a different glimpse of magic. I was in a rainforest with an Aboriginal guide. He was explaining to me the beliefs, the knowledge, the no-longer-secrets that his ancestors had held in their home, this ancient, dark cathedral forest that had turned tourist attraction. In the dim half-light covered by leafy canopy, he spoke and I listened as he explained how this plant was used for medicine, that one for food, still another for shelter. We drank tea and ate damper (the local fired-cooked bread) still warm from the fire.

When it was time to leave, we stepped out of the forest, and I walked back to my car in the parking lot, squinting my eyes against the bright sun. The automobiles sounded oddly loud buzzing past, and I drove back to my hotel feeling glum and pensive. I couldn't fathom why the experience had left me this way, but I suspected it had something to do with my lost connection to this earth. I was already missing the feeling of comfort this man had in the forest, his home. I returned to my room and, not knowing what to do with myself, decided to go for a run.

I ran on a trail that flirted with the border of the forest, sometimes crossing in, sometimes out. Though I couldn't see them, the ocean and the Great Barrier Reef were also near, just across the main road in the other direction. These two incredible natural habitats—the forest and the reef—were so alluring, yet so impenetrable.

As the trail wound away from the hotel, it grew quiet. I began to feel a return to that primeval place I had left a few hours before. The smell of burning vegetation hung heavy in the already hot, thick air. I heard birds squawking, insects trilling. The birds grew louder. I felt something brush my head, looked up but saw nothing. Then, another brush with a loud shriek this time. The birds were dive-bombing me. I looked up again, saw several circling. Then, again, I was the target. They were swooping close enough that I had to duck. What was going on? I ran faster—wait, that won't help—then slower. Then faster again.

I looked for a nest, for something to explain why I was a threat to these birds. There was a marsh nearby and what looked like a small pond with an island in the middle. The birds seemed to be coming from there. I assumed there was a nest there, but I couldn't tell for sure. I ran faster and faster, fascinated, frightened. It's ridiculous, I thought, to be scared of some birds. But their attack brought them close enough that I could feel their beaks on my scalp through my hair, though I tried to wave them off with my arms. The trail finally wound away from the water, and with that, the birds' cries grew more distant. The swooping stopped. I slowed and looked back, saw them circling higher in the sky now, and continued to run.

I'm still not sure what the message was that surreal day running in the forest, but I've thought about it a lot since then. "You don't really belong here," was the thought that kept repeating itself in my head. As if the birds were waking me from some romanticized jungle reverie and telling me to go back home and find significance in my own world.

Sometimes the message you get while running on the trail is clear, and other times it's not. I remember that trail-running incident in Australia precisely because it wasn't clear, because my mind was muddled and amazed at the same time, and because it has provided food for thought for years since. Whatever it was, one thing I'm sure of—it was a magical run in a wondrous place, both hostile and inviting at the same time.

More recently I found magic on the trail while researching and writing this book. Since I'd never been exposed to the world of ultra running, a friend invited me to pace her at a 100-miler, the Leadville Trail 100. I've tried just about every kind of running in the course of my career, but ultras had always seemed too much, too crazy—just not appealing. But pacing her for 25 miles or so sounded sane enough, and I agreed that the learning experience would be good for me, and good for this book.

When my friend reached the 50-mile mark, she had been running for more than 12 hours straight, and she was only halfway to the finish. And as my job as a pacer—running with her, offering emotional support and conversation, carrying Pop-Tarts and Gu—began, I only felt more convinced that these ultras were silly endeavors for a fringe element of die-hard runners.

But something happened along the way. As another friend and I traded off running with her for the last 50 miles, our ridiculous quest became clearer. We ran through the night, a clear and cold one up above 10,000 feet in Colorado's Rocky Mountains. We hiked fast up the hills and jogged slow on the downhills. She sucked down water, sports drinks, Coke, and animal crackers as I attempted to keep her spirits up. But since I wasn't used to running at 3:00 A.M., as often as not it was she who provided the conversation and encouragement. We had rough patches where she could barely put one foot in front of the other. We had strong spells where we passed other runners at what was essentially a blazing plod.

As we pressed on, we neared a point where we could just barely make out the glowsticks illuminating the trail up ahead. After climbing more than a thousand vertical feet, when we looked up, the little green lights hung from tree branches blended with the stars above until we couldn't tell where the glowsticks stopped and the stars began. The trail seemed to climb straight up to the sky.

And then we heard the music. As it grew louder we saw twinkles of light. The trail broke from its narrow confines and spilled out onto a dirt road. The mirage grew closer, until we were surrounded by sweet strains of opera. In the middle of the night, in the middle of nowhere, someone had decorated their house with holiday lights and set up outdoor speakers to serenade the silent stream of lonely runners. It was magical. We kept moving, the lights and the music growing fainter, until all was dark and silent again. And we wondered if we had imagined the whole thing.

By the time dawn broke, we realized that my friend would likely finish the race, her holy grail for the year. She'd been training since last year's race, when a storm at the top of the mountain had caught her unprepared and forced her to drop out. This year she'd done her homework. She'd done her training. The weather gods were kind. And we friends were there to share her triumph. Renee crossed that finish line wearing a smile and tears and the dirt and sweat of 100 miles. She was glad it was over—yet was already planning her next race. And I finally understood why.

By the time we'd finished, even this seemingly crazy trail-running event had come clear to me. Just keep putting one foot in front of the other. Just keep moving toward completion. Why not choose goals that are glorious and heroic? Why not do what is seemingly impossible? Why not seek out some magic? For some it may come in a 100-mile race. For others, though, it can come by just getting out the door and onto the trails beyond the backyard. In a way it's just a trail run, and in a way it's so much more. It's everything you thought you could never do—and now know that you can.

Trail Runner's Resource Guide

ORGANIZATIONS

**All American
Trail Running Association**

Box 9454

Colorado Springs, CO 80932

(719) 573-4405

www.trailrunner.com

**American Running
Association**

4405 East-West Highway

Suite 405

Bethesda, MD 20814

(800) 776-ARFA

www.americanrunning.org

**American Ultrarunning
Association**

4 Strawberry Lane

Morristown, NJ 07960

(973) 898-1261

www.americanultra.org

Road Runners Club of America

510 North Washington Street

Alexandria, Virginia 22314

(703) 836-0558

www.rrca.org

Running USA

5522 Camino Cerralvo

Santa Barbara, CA 93111

(805) 964-0608

www.runningusa.com

USA Track & Field

One RCA Dome, Suite 140

Indianapolis, IN 46225

(317) 261-0500

www.usatf.org

CLOTHING, SHOES, EQUIPMENT

Campmor

28 Parkway, Box 700

Upper Saddle River, NJ 07458-0700

(800) 525-4784

www.campmor.com

Eastbay

P.O. Box 8066

Wausau, WI 54402-8066

(800) 826-2205

www.eastbay.com

Road Runner Sports

5549 Copley Drive

San Diego, CA 92111

(800) 636-3560

www.roadrunnersports.com

Sierra Trading Post
5025 Campstool Road
Cheyenne, WY 82007-1898
(800) 713-4534
www.sierratradingpost.com

BOOKS

Beyond the Marathon: Trail Ultrarunning
by Robert B. Boeder
Old Mountain Press, 1996

50 Trail Runs in Southern California
by Stan Swartz, Jim Wolff, and
Samir Shahin, M.D.
The Mountaineers Books, 2000

Runner's World Complete Book of Running
edited by Amby Burfoot
Rodale, 1997

Runner's World Complete Book of Women's Running
by Dagny Scott
Rodale, 2000

Trail Runners Guide to Colorado
by Phil Mislinski, Monique Cole, and
Scott Boulbol
Fulcrum Publishers, 1999

Trail Running: From Novice to Master
by Kirsten Poulin, Stan Swartz, and
Christina Flaxel, M.D.
The Mountaineers Books, 2002

The Ultimate Guide to Trail Running
by Adam Chase and Nancy Hobbs
The Lyons Press, 2001

PUBLICATIONS

Runner's World magazine
Rodale
33 East Minor Street
Emmaus, PA 18098
(610) 967-5171
www.runnersworld.com

Trail Runner magazine
Big Stone Publishing
1101 Village Road UL-4D
Carbondale, CO 81623
(970) 704-1442
www.trailrunnermag.com

UltraRunning magazine
P.O. Box 890238
Weymouth, MA 02189-0238
(781) 340-0616
www.ultrarunning.com

WEB SITES OF INTEREST

www.acsm.org
Sports medicine information from the American College of Sports Medicine

www.active.com
Race information and registration

www.letsrun.com
Running news and message board

www.mountainrunning.com
Trail running in Canada and beyond

www.runningnetwork.com
Running and racing news

www.trailrunningusa.com
Online forum and news for trail runners

www.wilderness-survival.net
Safety, plants, animals, and general outdoor information

TRAIL-RUNNING IMAGES

Many of the images in this book were provided by PatitucciPhoto, the husband and wife team of Dan and Janine Patitucci. Specializing in mountain sports photography, the two also participate in the sports they photograph, most notably trail running.

More of their work may be seen on the Web site www.patitucciphoto.com.

Index

Boldface page references indicate photographs. <u>Underscored</u> references indicate boxed text.